Business Diplomacy

Riordan and Zhang share the skills, techniques, and mindsets used by diplomats in both Western and Chinese contexts, and adapt them to the needs of executives and multinational corporations (MNCs).

Their guide employs real-life case studies in understanding the international business environment and:

- Examines the shift to multipolarity and the rise of permacrisis and policrisis
- Highlights the long-term approach of diplomatic strategy and how it may be applied to business
- Provides a framework for companies to understand geopolitical risks
- Offers techniques to build resilience via network-building and coalitions

Engaging with topics such as cybersecurity, the re-shoring/friend-shoring phenomenon, and the evolution of technology companies as geopolitical actors, the authors demonstrate how the diplomat's perspective offers insights to companies looking to navigate the increasingly complex geopolitical environments of international trade and investments.

With an emphasis on practical guidance, this book would interest business executives and strategy planners, as well as diplomats and government officials.

Shaun Riordan is a senior advisor on public diplomacy to UNDP Saudi Arabia. He is a research fellow of the Chahar Institute in China and a senior consultant on digital, cyber, and public diplomacy with UNITAR. He has been a visiting fellow of the Netherlands Institute of International Relations ('Clingendael') and the London School of Economics. Shaun served for 16 years as a British diplomat with postings in New York, Taiwan, Beijing, and Madrid, as well as in the United Nations, Counter-Terrorism and Eastern Adriatic departments of the Foreign and Commonwealth Office in London. He has taught at diplomatic academies in Romania, the Dominican Republic, Bulgaria, and Spain.

Zhang Xiaotong is Professor of International Relations at KIMEP University in Almaty, Kazakhstan, where he also serves as Director of the university's China and Central Asia Studies Center (CCASC). Before entering academia, he spent 12 years in government service, including six years posted abroad in Brussels as Trade Attaché at the Mission of China to the European Union. After returning from Brussels, he worked at the U.S. Desk of China's Ministry of Commerce. Prior to joining KIMEP, he was Professor at Wuhan University and Fudan University, China. He currently serves as Editor-in-Chief of the journal *Economic Diplomacy*.

Business Diplomacy

A Business Executive's Guide to an Uncertain World

Shaun Riordan and Zhang Xiaotong

Routledge
Taylor & Francis Group
LONDON AND NEW YORK

Designed cover image: Getty Images

First published 2026
by Routledge
4 Park Square, Milton Park, Abingdon, Oxon OX14 4RN

and by Routledge
605 Third Avenue, New York, NY 10158

Routledge is an imprint of the Taylor & Francis Group, an informa business

British Library Cataloguing-in-Publication Data
A catalogue record for this book is available from the British Library

ISBN: 978-1-032-62507-2 (hbk)
ISBN: 978-1-032-62506-5 (pbk)
ISBN: 978-1-032-62508-9 (ebk)

DOI: 10.4324/9781032625089

Typeset in Optima
by Apex CoVantage, LLC

Contents

Introduction

Thriving through Turbulence: Why Business Leaders Must Think Like Diplomats

In September 2020, one of the co-authors of this book was approached by a Chinese multinational company eager to develop their business in Europe. The company was encouraged by the anticipated signing of the Comprehensive Agreement on Investment (CAI) between the European Union and China. Interpreting this development as a favourable strategic juncture, the company resolved to advance its expansion plans in Europe with determination.

However, just six months later, the EU imposed sanctions on China over alleged human rights abuses in Xinjiang under its newly established Global Human Rights Sanctions Regime. Beijing swiftly retaliated by sanctioning members of the European Parliament and the Council of the European Union – key decision-makers in the ratification of the CAI. As a result, the investment agreement was frozen indefinitely, dashing the Chinese company's optimism. Stunned by the abrupt turn of events, they had to reconsider their business strategy, now faced with an increasingly unpredictable geopolitical landscape.

This case illustrates a broader reality: economic statecraft is becoming an unavoidable factor in corporate decision-making. Beyond traditional trade wars and tariffs, governments are wielding legal, regulatory, and financial tools to advance national interests – often at the expense of businesses caught in the crossfire.

A striking example of this dynamic is the case of Frédéric Pierucci, a former Alstom executive, whose story is detailed in his book *The American Trap* (Pierucci & Aron, 2019). In 2013, Pierucci was arrested by U.S. authorities under the Foreign Corrupt Practices Act (FCPA) and imprisoned for nearly two years. His detention coincided with a broader U.S. investigation into Alstom, a major French energy and transport conglomerate, which ultimately resulted in the company selling its energy division to General Electric. Many observers saw this as a form of economic coercion – leveraging legal instruments to weaken a foreign competitor and enable an American corporate takeover. The case sent a chilling message to multinational companies: political and legal risks can be just as decisive as market forces in shaping business outcomes.

DOI: 10.4324/9781032625089-1

Both the Chinese company's experience in Europe and Alstom's downfall at the hands of U.S. economic statecraft underscore a fundamental reality of today's global economy: business is no longer just about supply chains, consumer demand, or financial performance. It is increasingly intertwined with great power rivalry and economic statecraft, where corporate decisions must account for the strategic calculations of states. Whether navigating investment agreements, sanctions, regulatory scrutiny, or extraterritorial legal risks, companies must adapt to a world where diplomacy and business are inseparable.

••

Our world is undergoing a profound transformation, marked by increasing uncertainty, volatility, and geopolitical realignments. Chinese President Xi Jinping has described this period as 'Profound Changes Unseen in a Century' (百年未有之大变局) (Xi, 2017) – a phrase that underscores China's view that the global order is experiencing a fundamental shift, similar to the seismic geopolitical changes brought about by major historical transitions, such as the First World War. Xi's perspective is deeply rooted in China's historical narrative: he sees the world moving away from Western-centric globalization and towards a multipolar order, where China plays a central role in shaping global governance.

Similarly, German Chancellor Olaf Scholz has characterized this moment as a 'Global Zeitenwende' – a turning point in world history (Scholz, 2022). This German term, meaning a historic paradigm shift, was first used by Scholz in response to Russia's invasion of Ukraine, which he saw as a watershed moment that shattered post-Cold War assumptions about European security. But beyond the war, Scholz's Zeitenwende reflects a broader realization that globalization is fragmenting under the pressures of geopolitics, supply chain disruptions, and ideological conflicts between authoritarian and democratic states. Both Xi and Scholz acknowledge a new era – but while China sees this as an opportunity to redefine global power structures, Germany, and the West, view it as a call to defend liberal values and economic resilience.

Policymakers and business leaders alike are now operating in a state of perpetual crisis management. From financial instability and pandemics to geopolitical conflicts and technological disruptions, uncertainty is no longer an occasional challenge – it is the 'New Normal'.

The Russo-Ukrainian War exemplifies this volatility. Few business executives anticipated this war. Companies exited Russia en masse. The world that businesses once relied on – one of open markets and predictable globalization – no longer exists. The liberal international order is being shattered as national security concerns override economic efficiency.

Globalization, once seen as an irreversible force, is now confronted with unprecedented challenges. In the United States, policymakers are openly questioning the economic orthodoxy that shaped global trade for decades.

Jake Sullivan (2023), the U.S. National Security Advisor under Joe Biden, proposed a 'New Washington Consensus', advocating for a return to industrial policy, supply chain security, and 'friend-shoring' – a direct response to China's rise as a technological and economic competitor. Robert Lighthizer (2023), U.S. Trade Representative during the first Trump administration, dismissed the idea of free trade, declaring that 'No trade is free!' He sees China as America's greatest geopolitical threat, describing China's economic system as 'Twenty-First-Century Mercantilism' (Lighthizer, 2023, pp. 89–111). Donald Trump continued his signature global tariff war into his second term.

These shifts in U.S. policy are not isolated. The European Union, Japan, and other advanced economies are increasingly adopting more defensive trade policies and securing strategic industries – a sign that economic nationalism is eroding and replacing the old model of interdependence. MNCs are trapped in the middle of this economic securitization.

Every time tensions escalate, companies operating in both countries find themselves in a precarious position, fearing that they will become collateral damage in tit-for-tat economic retaliation. During the U.S.–China trade war, nearly all major American and Chinese MNCs faced disruptions – whether through tariffs, export controls, or heightened scrutiny from regulators.

ZTE's near-collapse in 2018 was an early warning sign. The Chinese telecom giant was accused of violating U.S. sanctions against Iran and North Korea, leading the U.S. Department of Commerce to impose an export ban that cut ZTE off from critical American-made components. The ban was so severe that it was seen as a corporate death sentence – only lifted after Xi Jinping personally intervened with then-President Donald Trump (Trump, 2018). The price of survival was steep: ZTE was forced to fire half of its executives, accept a U.S.-appointed compliance officer, and pay a $1 billion fine.

ZTE's case set a precedent for future U.S. economic measures against Chinese firms, including Huawei and TikTok, and semiconductor restrictions, demonstrating that businesses can no longer separate commercial decisions from geopolitical realities.

If 2018 was a watershed moment for U.S.–China relations, the broader transformation had already begun a decade earlier, in 2008. Since the financial crisis, the international economic and business systems have faced a cascade of shocks and disruptions: the Global Financial Crisis shattered confidence in Western-led financial markets. Brexit in 2016 challenged the assumptions of regional economic integration. The U.S.–China trade war in 2018 fractured global supply chains. The COVID-19 pandemic (2020–2022) exposed the vulnerabilities of hyper-globalized trade. Russia's invasion of Ukraine further disrupted global energy markets and security architecture. Renewed conflict in the Persian Gulf in 2026 has threatened the security of the Strait of Hormuz, disrupting global travel and energy flows.

The cumulative effect of these crises has led to an ever more uncertain and volatile international geo-economic environment. Companies must now navigate a world of heightened risk, geopolitical interference, and economic fragmentation.

Now, business leaders, policymakers, and scholars must grapple with a fundamental question: how can companies thrive in an era where war, diplomacy, and business are increasingly inseparable? The answers to this question will define the future of international commerce.

••

With the dramatic changes on global scenes comes the rise of business diplomacy. We are witnessing a profound transformation in the global economic and political landscape, where businesses can no longer remain neutral observers. The return of geopolitics; the fragmentation of globalization; and the weaponization of trade, technology, and finance have forced MNCs to rethink their strategies. Business diplomacy has emerged as a critical tool – not just for securing market access but also for navigating geopolitical risks, building strategic alliances, and ensuring corporate survival in an increasingly uncertain world.

I.1 What is Business Diplomacy?

We define Business Diplomacy as the adoption by multinational corporations and executives of the techniques, skills, and mindsets of diplomats in managing the uncertainty and volatility of the 21st-century international business environment. It bridges the gap between the corporate world and international politics, requiring business leaders to adopt the tactics, negotiation techniques, and risk management skills of professional diplomats.

Business diplomacy is often confused with similar concepts such as commercial, economic or corporate diplomacy. Commercial diplomacy is conducted by the commercial sections of embassies or government agencies to support trade and investment facilitation for businesses. Economic diplomacy is a state-led effort to acquire economic intelligence, negotiate trade agreements, and use economic tools for diplomatic leverage (Woolcock, 2025, pp. 7-9). Corporate diplomacy focuses on internal corporate governance, particularly managing headquarters–subsidiary relationships and corporate social responsibility (CSR) initiatives. Business diplomacy is practised directly by MNCs (often with the help of consultants, former diplomats, or military officers) to navigate international regulations, geopolitical risks, and government relations. While commercial and economic diplomacies focus on government-led initiatives, business diplomacy is corporate-driven, helping companies anticipate, adapt, and influence geopolitical dynamics.

Individuals with diplomatic, governmental, or intelligence background often assist business executives in practising business diplomacy, particularly in countries where the 'revolving door' system allows senior officials to transition into corporate advisory roles. This is especially true in the United States and parts of Europe, where former diplomats and policymakers help companies navigate geopolitical uncertainty, regulatory scrutiny, and cross-border negotiations. Increasingly, Asian and other emerging markets are recognizing the value of business diplomacy, integrating it into corporate strategies to cope with economic statecraft, sanctions, and shifting trade policies.

I.2 Past Studies of Business Diplomacy

The earliest conceptualizations of business diplomacy emerged from corporate–government relations literature, emphasizing how firms interact with diplomats, policymakers, and trade negotiators to advance commercial interests. Saner and Yiu (2003) defined business diplomacy as the adaptation of diplomatic techniques to corporate strategy, particularly in stakeholder engagement, lobbying, and conflict resolution. Westermann-Behaylo et al. (2015) extended this view by examining how MNCs mediate tensions between governments, civil society, and trade unions, while Muldoon (2005) analysed business diplomacy through the lens of CSR, arguing that firms use diplomatic practices to build legitimacy and mitigate reputational risks. While these studies established the importance of corporate–government engagement, they were premised on a relatively stable global order in which firms could shape regulations through soft power and strategic negotiation. They did not anticipate a world in which geopolitical tensions would fundamentally reshape the rules of global trade and investment.

In the 2010s, scholarship expanded to consider how business diplomacy plays out in conflict zones, emerging markets, and fragile states. Henisz (2014) argued that MNCs operating in unstable regions often act as de facto diplomats, engaging in peacebuilding and crisis management to safeguard their operations. Gertz (2018) explored how firms manage political risks in Africa, the Middle East, and Latin America, showing how they form alliances with local governments and navigate informal power structures. Riordan (2019) further suggested that business diplomacy must involve negotiations not only with state actors but also with non-state actors such as insurgent groups, militias, and NGOs. These contributions broadened the scope of business diplomacy, but they remained too region-specific and did not fully capture how great-power rivalries, sanctions, and systemic decoupling now directly impact even firms operating in stable markets like Europe, North America, and East Asia.

This gap is particularly evident in the age of economic statecraft (Baldwin, 1985; Zhang, 2024), where global trade and technology are weaponized (Farrell & Newman, 2019). Much of the literature focuses on micro-level engagement – regulatory approvals, CSR initiatives, or trade facilitation – without accounting for the fact that businesses have become geopolitical pawns in great-power competition. The U.S.–China technology conflict illustrates this point: cases such as Huawei and ZTE demonstrate that business diplomacy is no longer about corporate–government dialogue but about survival in a system where governments deliberately target firms for strategic reasons. Huawei's exclusion from Western 5G networks and the restrictions imposed under the U.S. CHIPS Act reveal that corporations can no longer assume neutrality; they are increasingly aligned – or forced into alignment – with national interests.

Another gap in the past literature is its neglect of the ideological dimension of business diplomacy. Previous studies assumed that firms could navigate politics through alliances and lobbying, but the current reality shows that ideology and values matter as much as economics. Sanctions and entity lists illustrate this shift: hundreds of Chinese companies have been added to U.S. defence and commerce blacklists not solely for legal violations but also for political and ideological reasons such as human rights concerns. Likewise, Western companies in China face backlash over their stances on Taiwan, Xinjiang, and Hong Kong, indicating that corporate diplomacy is now deeply politicized.

Finally, earlier studies often assumed that globalization would continue to expand, enabling MNCs to operate seamlessly across borders. In reality, the fragmentation of global supply chains and the rise of regional trade blocs have made this assumption obsolete. Supply chain diplomacy during the U.S.–China trade war illustrates how firms are compelled to reconfigure production networks, shifting operations from China to Vietnam, India, or Mexico. Business diplomacy today thus involves navigating a fractured global economy where alignment with new regional structures is as important as global expansion once was.

I.3 Towards a New Business Diplomacy Framework

Given the shortcomings of the existing literature, we need a new business diplomacy paradigm that (1) moves beyond corporate–government lobbying to address geo-economic warfare, sanctions, and forced market exits; (2) recognizes that MNCs are now geopolitical actors, not just commercial players; (3) accounts for ideological battles – where businesses face risks based on their perceived national affiliations, supply chain ethics, and regulatory alignments; and (4) incorporates the weaponization of trade and technology, acknowledging that businesses are at the centre of great-power rivalries.

••

The core of business diplomacy lies in managing *geopolitical risks*, ensuring that companies can not only survive but also thrive in an increasingly volatile global environment. In an interconnected world, where political tensions, economic sanctions, trade wars, and military conflicts frequently disrupt business operations, companies must navigate these uncertainties with strategic foresight. Business diplomacy, therefore, requires an understanding of geopolitics, which, at its heart, is about interstate competition for power, influence, and resources.

Geopolitical risks have a direct impact on business operations. These risks have become increasingly prominent in recent years, forcing thousands of Western companies to withdraw from Russia and placing hundreds of Chinese high-tech and state-owned enterprises on the U.S. Department of Defense and Department of Commerce's Entity List. Effectively managing these risks is at the core of business diplomacy.

Diplomats and soldiers are trained to tackle geopolitical risks. Their daily work deals with forecasting, analysing, and mitigating geopolitical risks. They have a clear mission and a strong sense of duty. For them, international affairs is not just a field of study but also a vocation. They are equipped with the skills necessary to analyse the world situation, manage crises, negotiate under pressure, and build effective networks. Day and night, they work on the frontlines, engaging with the most sensitive information and reporting back to capitals the most up-to-date intelligence and policy recommendations. They have an instinct for sensing crisis and work hard to avoid escalation.

Therefore, their approach, skills, and experiences are highly valuable for business executives, who are faced with an increasingly turbulent geopolitical environment. That is why business diplomacy is no longer optional for MNCs but a necessity. MNCs have become geopolitical actors, whether they choose to recognize it or not. Corporate strategy can no longer be confined to markets and management; it must integrate diplomatic tools, political risk assessment, and crisis management. Business diplomacy is about corporate survival in an era where geopolitics and economic statecraft define the rules of global commerce. In the coming decades, those who master business diplomacy – thinking like diplomats while acting as business leaders – will be the ones who endure and prosper in a world where the weaponization of economics has become the new normal.

••

We have two goals in this book. First, we want to equip business executives with a diplomatic approach to managing geopolitical risks and developing their global strategy. Second, we want to explain how to practise business diplomacy in two most sensitive and vulnerable areas of international business, that is cyber, and high-tech.

In the first part of this book, we want to promote a diplomatic approach to managing uncertainty and volatility that can be adapted to the needs of companies and their executives. Diplomats and foreign policy officers constantly manage crises long before the stability of international business environment starts to erode. They went through the Cold War and managed the interdependence within the West and between the West and East in 1990s and early 21st century. Through the first four chapters, we will explain that there is a distinctive diplomatic approach to international affairs (Chapter 1), how to adapt this diplomatic approach to business strategies (Chapter 2), how a business can develop its own geopolitical risk analysis (Chapter 3), and how companies build global networks among state and non-state actors and stakeholders (Chapter 4).

In the second part of this book, we want to focus on the two most sensitive and vulnerable areas which desperately need the help of business diplomacy, namely, cyber and high-tech. Throughout the following chapters, we will explain how to engage with governments and other actors to enhance cybersecurity (Chapter 5) and how to adopt a diplomacy of technology companies for engaging with governments and international organizations (Chapter 6).

••

We strongly feel that doing business is like doing diplomacy. Business executives need to act like diplomats. What makes this book distinctive is that it is written jointly by an ex-Chinese and an ex-British diplomat – *East meets West*. This dual perspective not only enriches our analysis of business diplomacy and geopolitical risk management but also reflects the reality that international business operates at the intersection of different cultures, political systems, and strategic traditions.

References

Baldwin, David A. (1985). *Economic statecraft*. Princeton: Princeton University Press.

Caldara, D., & Iacoviello, M. (2018). *Measuring geopolitical risk* [International finance discussion papers, 1222, Board of Governors of the Federal Reserve System].

Farrell, H., & Newman, A. L. (2019). Weaponized interdependence: How global economic networks shape state coercion. *International Security, 44*(1), 42–79. https://doi.org/10.1162/isec_a_00351

Flint, C. (2017). *Introduction to geopolitics* (3rd ed.). Routledge.

Flint, C. (2022). *Introduction to geopolitics* (4th ed.). Routledge.

Gertz, G. (2018). Commercial diplomacy and political risk in the internationalization of firms. *International Business Review, 27*(5), 1148–1157.

Henisz, W. J. (2014). *Corporate diplomacy: Building reputations and relationships with external stakeholders*. Routledge.

Lighthizer, R. (2023). *No trade is free: Changing course, taking on China, and helping America's workers*. HarperCollins.

Muldoon, J. P. (2005). The diplomacy of business. *Diplomacy & Statecraft, 16*(2), 341–359.

Pierucci, F., & Aron, M. (2019). *The American trap: My battle to expose America's secret economic war against the rest of the world*. Hodder & Stoughton.

Reuters. (2018, May 13). *Trump says working with China's Xi to help ZTE get back into business*.

Riordan, S. (2019). Business diplomacy: Shaping the firm's geopolitical risk environment. In N. Bayne & S. Woolcock (Eds.), *The new economic diplomacy* (pp. 201–217). Routledge.

Saner, R., & Yiu, L. (2003). Business diplomacy management: A core competency for global companies. *Academy of Management Perspectives, 14*(1), 80–92.

Scholz, O. (2022, February 27). *Policy statement by Olaf Scholz, Chancellor of the Federal Republic of Germany, at the special session of the German Bundestag*. The Federal Government of Germany. https://www.bundesregierung.de/breg-en/service/archive/policy-statement-by-olaf-scholz-chancellor-of-the-federal-republic-of-germany-and-member-of-the-german-bundestag-27-february-2022-in-berlin-2008378

Sullivan, J. (2023, April 27). *Remarks by national security advisor Jake Sullivan on renewing American economic leadership at the Brookings Institution* [Speech]. The White House. https://www.whitehouse.gov/briefing-room/speeches-remarks/2023/04/27/remarks-by-national-security-advisor-jake-sullivan-on-renewing-american-economic-leadership-at-the-brookings-institution/

Trump, D. J. (2018, May 13). *President Xi of China, and I, are working together to give massive Chinese phone company, ZTE, a way to get back into business, fast* [Tweet]. X (formerly Twitter). https://twitter.com/realDonaldTrump/status/995680316458262533.

Westermann-Behaylo, M., Rehbein, K., & Fort, T. L. (2015). Enhancing the concept of corporate diplomacy: Encompassing political corporate social responsibility, international business, and peace through commerce. *Academy of Management Perspectives*, *29*(4), 387–404.

Woolcock, S. (2025). *The new economic diplomacy: Decision-making and negotiation in international economic relations* (5th ed.). Routledge.

Xi, J. (2017, October 18). *Secure a decisive victory in building a moderately prosperous society in all respects and strive for the great success of socialism with Chinese characteristics for a new era: Report to the 19th National Congress of the Communist Party of China*. Foreign Languages Press.

Zhang, X., & Xu, Z. (2020). "一带一路"海外重大项目的地缘政治风险与应对——概念与理论构建 [BRI projects' geopolitical risks: Concepts and theorization]. *Global Review*, *12*(3), 80–96.

Zhang, X. (2024). *The new economic statecraft: China, the United States and the European Union*. Routledge.

1 The Diplomatic Approach to International Relations

For three decades following the end of the Cold War, diplomacy and diplomats focused on promoting economic prosperity. The logic of globalization and interdependence led diplomats to move away from their traditional emphasis on war and peace to engage in economic diplomacy. The Global Financial Crisis in 2008 further underscored the need for diplomacy to support economic objectives such as reviving the global economy. The Obama Administration emphasized economic statecraft as a key component of U.S. foreign policy, using diplomacy and global presence to strengthen economy at home (Clinton, 2011). China did something similar. The then Chinese President Hu Jintao stated in the context of the Global Financial Crisis,

> Diplomatic work should take as an important task the effective response to the impact of the international financial crisis, the maintenance of steady and relatively fast economic development, and serving the goals of ensuring growth, safeguarding people's livelihood, and maintaining stability.
>
> (Ministry of Foreign Affairs of the People's Republic of China, 2009)

However, the global security situation has deteriorated significantly in recent years. Rising geopolitical tensions, strategic competition between major powers, and regional conflicts have reshaped the role of diplomacy. Instead of simply fostering economic globalization, diplomats increasingly find themselves navigating a landscape of heightened economic competition and confrontation. Economic diplomacy has now evolved into what is often referred to as 'economic statecraft' (Zhang, 2024), emphasizing the power play (Okano-Heijmans, 2013, p. 19) and coercive measures aimed at advancing national strategic interests.

As diplomats contend with a worsening political and economic landscape, businesses are also struggling to adapt to these new challenges. MNCs faced immense pressure and operational risks following Russia's invasion of Ukraine in February 2022. Many Western companies, from oil giants to consumer brands, had to make abrupt and costly decisions to withdraw from

DOI: 10.4324/9781032625089-2

the Russian market. Some faced asset seizures, financial losses, and supply chain disruptions. The total losses incurred by companies withdrawing from Russia were estimated in the hundreds of billions of dollars, demonstrating how international business is no longer insulated from geopolitical tensions.

Now, business executives are adapting to a new geopolitical reality. International politics has become a major variable in corporate decision-making, impacting everything from supply chain strategies to market entry plans. The growing interaction between politics and business requires a diplomatic approach to managing international businesses. Companies must now assess geopolitical risks as part of their strategic planning, navigate complex geo-economic environments, and engage with governments more proactively to safeguard their interests.

This is why we believe that a diplomatic approach to international business is essential for today's executives. Understanding global power dynamics, economic statecraft, and the interplay between politics and markets is no longer optional – it is a necessity. By integrating diplomatic thinking into business strategy, companies can better navigate an increasingly realist world, anticipate risks, and seize opportunities in a complex international environment.

1.1 What Is the Diplomatic Approach to International Relations?

Diplomats are official representatives of their home country, who work to manage international relations and protect national interests. They operate in various capacities, including negotiation, policy analysis, crisis management, cultural exchange, and public diplomacy. Their work spans across embassies, consulates, international organizations, and government agencies.

If we quickly compare diplomats and entrepreneurs, you will see quite a few differences (see Table 1.1). Diplomats safeguard national interests,

Table 1.1 The Differences between Diplomats and Entrepreneurs

Dimension	*Diplomats/Foreign Service Officers*	*Entrepreneurs*
Objective	Safeguard national interests, promote foreign policy	Pursue business profits, expand market share
Decision Logic	Long-term thinking, incremental negotiation	Fast decision-making, high-risk, high-reward
Stakeholders	National governments, international organizations, NGOs	Shareholders, investors, customers, competitors
Negotiation Style	Compromise and balance, soft power utilization	Competition and execution, hard power application
Operational Environment	Political environments, legal systems, international relations	Market trends, consumer demands, industry competition

while entrepreneurs drive business interests. The former focus on long-term geopolitical dynamics between nations, while the latter emphasize market competition and profit growth. Diplomats pursue long-term balance, emphasizing incremental negotiations and cooperation, while entrepreneurs seek rapid growth, focusing on competition and market adaptation. Diplomats tend to minimize conflicts, maintain stability, and avoid extreme or high-risk decisions, as such choices may lead to crises or catastrophes that a country or the international community cannot bear. In contrast, entrepreneurs are often willing to assume high risks in exchange for innovation and market breakthroughs. Diplomats' negotiation styles lean towards compromise and long-term influence, while entrepreneurs adopt a more direct, pragmatic approach focused on short-term gains. Diplomats serve the nation and the global system, while entrepreneurs serve the market and corporate stakeholders.

The vocation of diplomats is to manage world affairs. What sets them apart from other professionals is their keen professional instincts regarding the global context and their sensitivity to, and even affinity for, uncertainties, volatilities, and crises. They view themselves as key players on the world stage, representing national interests and safeguarding peace through proactive diplomacy. They understand that if diplomacy fails, war is the following consequence. Thus, diplomacy serves as the primary safety valve against war.

Specifically, diplomats manage world affairs through analysis, planning, negotiation, and socialization. To a large extent, the qualifications of a diplomat depend primarily on these essential qualities.

1.1.1 Strategic and Long-Term Thinking

Diplomats develop strategies to act rationally and pragmatically. However, rationality in diplomacy depends on strategic and long-term thinking, a key skill for diplomats.

In China's strategic thinking, a key concept is 'Shi' (势), which can be understood as strategic momentum, structural advantage, or alignment with historical trends. 'Shi' guides Chinese diplomats' understanding of international politics. Professor Zhu Linqun, from China's Foreign Affairs University, interpreted 'Shi' as follows: (1) The Distinctive Feature of the Times – the broad, defining trends that shape the international order, such as geopolitical shifts, economic transformations, and technological advancements. (2) The International Power Configuration (国际格局, guoji geju) – the distribution of power among major states, including the relative strength of great powers and emerging trends in global governance (Zhu, 2010).

China's diplomacy, in a nutshell, is the process of following 'Shi'. A key Chinese diplomatic principle, 'Shun Shi Er Wei' (顺势而为) – 'following the trend' – guides China's diplomatic approach. This means avoiding direct confrontation with the times, strategically positioning itself within the evolving global order, and ensuring alignment with global shifts. For example, Deng Xiaoping's reforms, starting in 1978, reflected a shift in *Shi* from revolution to economic development, leading to China's global integration in the prime time of globalization in the 1980s and 1990s. China's *Shi*-based strategy is flexible, long-term oriented, and responsive to change.

In *The Art of War*, Sun Tzu elevates the concept of *Shi* as the decisive factor in achieving victory. He explains,

> Warfare is the way of deception. Hence, when able, appear unable; when active, appear inactive; when near, appear far; when far, appear near. Thus, shaping the enemy's perception while remaining invisible yourself, and adapting to the enemy's changes to secure victory – this is called Shi.
>
> (Tzu, 1963)

This notion of *Shi* emphasizes the strategic use of emerging favourable conditions and the manipulation of the operational environment to gain advantage.

'Shi', as a key strategic concept, means a lot for companies in volatile times. It means companies need to have a sound understanding of the global context. A capable business executive who operates globally needs to be an expert in U.S.–China relations, as this relationship will define the global commercial landscape in the coming decades. Tim Cook, the CEO of Apple, has tried to achieve a balance between the two superpowers. On the one hand, Apple has shifted part of its production to India and Vietnam to reduce reliance on the Chinese market (Reuters, 2023). On the other hand, Apple has promised to increase investment in China (Reuters, 2024). Apple is hedging between the United States and China in an increasingly *bipolar* world.

As a senior business executive, he or she needs to know how many poles of power co-exist in the world. Are we living in a unipolar world, a bipolar world, or a multipolar world? This is indeed a Hamlet-like question. Yet it is an extremely important one because different configurations of poles in the global power structure lead to different patterns of state behaviour in foreign policy. Companies ultimately operate within these foreign policy frameworks and constraints. After the collapse of the USSR, the world entered a U.S.-dominant unipolar moment. China chose to join the U.S.-led international system and the global economy. It was eventually allowed to join the World Trade Organization and benefited tremendously. After the 2008 Global Financial Crisis, the United States suffered a relative decline, and China seized the opportunity to rise. This shift enabled China to pursue ambitious connectivity projects, such as the Belt and Road Initiative, translating decades of accumulated national wealth into global influence.

Business executives also need to understand the rhythms and paces of the global economy and international politics. Here, we offer a conceptual compass called 'Economic Long Waves and Hegemonic Cycles' (see

Figure 1.1). This analytical compass builds on the idea of Kondratiev Long Waves, first proposed by Nikolai Kondratiev, a Russian economist, in the 1920s. Kondratiev observed that the capitalist world economy experiences long-term economic cycles lasting roughly 50–60 years. Each long wave contains two phases: Phase A, characterized by economic expansion and rapid growth, and Phase B, marked by stagnation, restructuring, and crisis.

Although Kondratiev did not explain the key drivers behind these cycles, later scholars notably Joseph Schumpeter, argued that long waves are driven by waves of technological innovation. Schumpeter described this process as 'creative destruction', in which new technologies and industries disrupt existing economic structures and create new engines of growth.

These long economic waves also have profound political and geopolitical implications. As indicated in Figure 1.1, transitions between every long wave, or between Phase A (growth) and Phase B (stagnation), coincide with shifts in global power structures. These transitions, typically lasting for 5–10 years, witness wars, revolutions, and geopolitical disturbances.

Today, the world appears to be entering such a transitional moment, moving from the fifth Kondratieff wave towards a possible sixth wave driven by emerging technologies such as artificial intelligence, digital infrastructure, and advanced manufacturing. Recent geopolitical events – including major wars, technological competition, and disruptions in global supply chains – reflect this broader structural transition.

The concept of paired economic long waves and hegemonic cycles should not be treated as a strict predictive or scientific model. Rather, it serves as a strategic analytical framework that helps policymakers and business executives understand the broader rhythms of global change. Periods of technological

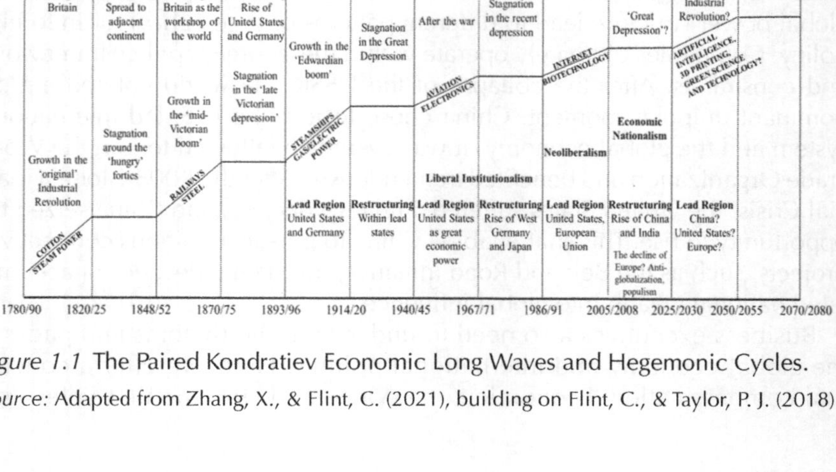

Figure 1.1 The Paired Kondratiev Economic Long Waves and Hegemonic Cycles.

Source: Adapted from Zhang, X., & Flint, C. (2021), building on Flint, C., & Taylor, P. J. (2018)

transformation tend to coincide with the rise and decline of great powers, the reshuffling of global power structures, and shifts in regional institutions and foreign policies.

In such an era of creative disruption, business executives cannot rely solely on traditional market analysis. They must also understand the geopolitical and technological forces reshaping the global system. Faced with structural changes in international politics (what the Chinese call 'Shi'), companies need to adapt quickly, build resilience, and develop strategies that respond to rapidly evolving global conditions.

1.1.2 Strategic Communication and Socializing

Diplomats understand that before striking any deal, the precondition is to build trust. Without trust, meaningful negotiations are nearly impossible. For diplomats, there exists an international community of professionals who share a common diplomatic mindset and frequently engage in social interactions. These interactions are not merely ceremonial but serve a strategic purpose. As Chinese diplomats like to put it, 'At critical moments, it is about finding the right people, having the right conversations, and making things happen' (State-owned Assets Supervision and Administration Commission of China, 2011). This underscores the essential role of trust and informal channels in diplomacy.

A key diplomatic skill is empathy – the ability to see a problem through the eyes of the other party, even a rival. This skill often results in diplomats being unfairly accused of 'going native' or sympathizing too much with the interests of a foreign government (Riordan, 2018, p. 75). However, the reality is that diplomats must constantly navigate between two perspectives: their home country's interests and the views of their counterparts. A successful diplomat seamlessly shifts between these two tables, ensuring alignment between domestic priorities and international realities.

One of the authors of this book still vividly remembers that, during a very difficult trade negotiation between China and the European Union involving 20 million jobs in China and 5 million jobs in Europe, he sat *tête-à-tête* with his European counterpart in the latter's office. When the negotiations remained stuck, the European counterpart reached to the bottom drawer of his desk and, to everyone's surprise, took out a bottle of wine despite the tense atmosphere. The mood immediately relaxed, and the negotiations began to move forward in a more constructive spirit.

In real negotiations, diplomats often have to test the bottom line of their counterparts, and this requires a high level of mutual trust because diplomats can only say what they are authorized to say. Yet in practice, in order to move negotiations forward and reach a deal, negotiators sometimes need to go slightly beyond their formal mandate, test the bottom line of the other side, and see how far both sides can go. All this requires a tremendous amount of trust and strong communication skills.

Case Study: Establishing and Launching the U.S.–China Strategic Economic Dialogue (SED)

When Henry Paulson became U.S. Treasury Secretary in 2006, he quickly realized that the growing economic interdependence between the United States and China required a more structured and high-level forum than the existing mechanisms. As he recounts in *Dealing with China*, he advocated for the creation of the U.S.–China SED as a regular platform to tackle complex issues like currency reform, trade imbalances, and market access (Paulson, 2015, p. 207).

Paulson understood, however, that institutional innovation alone would be insufficient. Trust and personal diplomacy would be critical. As he put it, '*Accomplishing this would require not just periodic official meetings but a continuous process of negotiation and* discussion *at ministry and agency levels to build trust and help defuse any crises that would inevitably arise*' (Paulson, 2015, p. 188).

Before the formal SED meetings began, Paulson invested significant time in cultivating relationships with key Chinese leaders, especially Vice Premier Wu Yi and Finance Minister Jin Renqing. One illustrative moment came during an informal dinner at Paulson's home in Washington, D.C., in May 2007. As tensions rose over the issue of financial sector equity caps, Paulson and Wu Yi stepped outside for a private, emotionally charged conversation. Paulson recalled:

> 'I took Wu Yi aside on the patio. . . . I was frustrated, and I got a little loud. . . . It got so heated that Wendy, who could hear us from inside, worried we wouldn't sit down together to eat. . . . But I could see that Wu Yi was still upset. . . . Sorry that I had upset her, I just put my arms around Wu Yi. . . . "Don't worry," I assured her. "This is going to be a success"'. (Paulson, 2015, pp. 212–213)

This moment underscored how personal interaction – even when difficult – could pave the way for deeper mutual understanding. Paulson emphasized that 'there was plenty we disagreed about, but we both valued the dialogue that allowed us to defuse crises and make progress on those areas where we could agree' (Paulson, 2015, p. 264). His respect for Wu Yi evolved into genuine professional affection:

> 'That was my introduction to China's Iron Lady, and the beginning of a soft spot in my heart for her . . . I felt an admiration for her that would shift over time into professional affection'. (Paulson, 2015, p. 196)

These trust-building efforts laid a critical foundation. When the SED officially launched in December 2006, it was not just an institutional achievement but also a product of sustained personal diplomacy. Reflecting on the experience, Paulson noted:

> 'As Treasury secretary, I had worked to build lasting relationships, this time between countries. . . . But with the SED we had created a forum for relations between our countries that would carry on after us'. (Paulson, 2015, p. 264)

Paulson was right. The establishment of the SED, and its later upgrade to the S&ED (Strategic and Economic Dialogue), created an important institutional platform for sustained engagement between China and the United States. Over time, this high-level dialogue helped build mutual confidence and expand practical cooperation. In 2014, the two countries agreed to grant each other's citizens ten-year multiple-entry visas (White House, 2014), a policy that significantly strengthened people-to-people exchanges and reinforced the foundation of China–U.S. interdependence. The Obama administration also rolled out the '100,000 Strong Initiative', which aimed to send more than 100,000 American students to study in China.

This case highlights how, in high-stakes diplomacy, informal and interpersonal engagement is indispensable. The ability to listen, respond empathetically, and develop trust over time can transform seemingly intractable disputes into areas of cooperation.

1.1.3 Negotiations

Diplomats negotiate. Negotiation, the art of securing agreements through strategic bargaining, lies at the core of diplomacy. The goal of negotiation is to find a win-set, which can mean achieving a win-win outcome or, at the very least, agreeing on the lowest common denominator to facilitate cooperation. The failure of negotiations can lead to war.

Diplomatic negotiations unfold within a complex structure that Robert Putnam describes as a 'two-level game' (Putnam, 1988). This framework requires diplomats to navigate two interconnected chessboards – one at the international level, where they negotiate with foreign counterparts, and another at the domestic level, where they must secure approval from political leaders, bureaucracies, and interest groups. Diplomats constantly navigate between the two levels. Success in diplomacy depends on a negotiator's ability to align these two dimensions, ensuring that international commitments are viable domestically.

At an operational level, diplomats use a range of negotiation tactics to enhance their bargaining power. Some of the most notable include the following: (1) Issue Linkage – connecting related or unrelated issues in negotiations to gain leverage. (2) Party linkage – introducing a third party to strengthen negotiation position. The EU's trade negotiations with China highlight the deliberate use of these bargaining tactics (Zhang, 2023).

Case Study: The EU–China Textiles Trade Negotiations

Rather than treating the surge of Chinese textile exports as a narrow trade conflict, the EU deliberately embedded the dispute within the broader context of the overall EU–China relationship. In other words, the negotiation was not only about textiles but also about the long-term political partnership between the two sides. As the Chinese leadership itself recognized during the crisis, 'China's relationship with the European Union is much broader than the textile case alone . . . we cannot allow the single textile issue to affect the China-EU comprehensive strategic partnership' (Zhang, 2023, p. 164). By framing the dispute in this wider diplomatic context, the EU effectively encouraged China to view concessions in the textile sector as a price worth paying for maintaining the overall strategic partnership.

At the same time, the EU also employed party linkage, strategically leveraging the presence of a third actor – the United States – in the negotiations. The EU and the United States were negotiating textile restrictions with China simultaneously, creating a triangular bargaining environment. EU Trade Commissioner Peter Mandelson tactically linked the EU negotiations with the parallel US–China talks to improve the EU's bargaining position. As documented in the negotiations, Mandelson explicitly signalled that the EU would provide China with a better offer than the United States, even instructing his team to revise the EU proposal to ensure it was 'better than the American one' (Zhang, 2023, p. 164).

This triangular strategy served two purposes. First, the EU implicitly leveraged US pressure to push China towards compromise. Second, by differentiating its approach from Washington's more confrontational stance, the EU was able to position itself as a more cooperative negotiating partner. In this way, linkage with the United States altered the balance of power in the negotiations and helped the EU secure concessions from China.

These cases show that the success of diplomacy often depends less on material power alone and more on the skilful manipulation of issues, alliances, and narratives to expand win-sets and reshape bargaining dynamics.

1.1.4 Crisis Management

Diplomats are inherently accustomed to navigating war and geopolitical tensions, making crisis management and emergency response a natural extension of their professional responsibilities. Negotiations and cross-cultural dialogues lie at the core of diplomacy, and crisis management represents the ultimate test of these daily engagements. However, crises demand more than routine negotiation skills; they require unique qualities such as adaptability, resilience, strategic foresight, and the ability to operate under extreme pressure. Diplomats are rigorously trained to handle such situations, serving as critical mediators in times of instability.

Case Study: U.S. and Allies' Response to Russia's Invasion of Ukraine

Following Russia's full-scale invasion of Ukraine in February 2022, the United States, in coordination with its NATO and G7 allies, launched an unprecedented diplomatic and economic response. Wally Adeyemo, then U.S. Under Secretary of the Treasury for International Affairs vividly detailed how American diplomats and policymakers coordinated with allies to impose severe economic sanctions on Russia, cutting it off from key financial systems and restricting its access to advanced technologies (Adeyemo, 2022).

This case illustrates that America's crisis management strategy consisted of three key steps: first, intelligence collection and the preparation of sanctions; second, coalition building through multilateral diplomacy; and third, the implementation of economic sanctions.

Unlike many of its European allies, the Biden administration was convinced at a very early stage that Russia would invade Ukraine. As Adeyemo revealed, 'In November, the U.S. intelligence community quickly shared the intelligence pointing to Russia's potential invasion with U.S. allies and partners in Europe and began laying the groundwork for the response' (Adeyemo, 2022).

Coalition building played a decisive role in the effectiveness of this strategy. As Adeyemo explained, 'To make this targeted strategy work, the Department of the Treasury had to work closely with a global coalition of allies and partners'. He further noted, 'From the outset, Biden and Yellen made multilateralism the foundation of our response to Russia'. The Biden administration demonstrated remarkable effectiveness in coalition building. In response to Russia's invasion of Ukraine, Washington worked closely with its partners to construct a multilayered sanctions coalition that included the G7, European allies, and a broader group of nearly 40 countries aligning their export controls and financial restrictions (Rogowsky, 2026). This multilevel coalition significantly amplified the impact of sanctions by limiting Russia's access to global financial markets, advanced technologies, and critical supply chains.

As Wally further explains, 'The overarching objective was clear: to degrade Russian President Vladimir Putin's ability to wage his illegal war'. This strategy combined several economic statecraft tools. Most notably, the United States imposed sweeping financial sanctions: 'We sanctioned Russia's key financial institutions, immobilized its central bank reserves, and cut off many of its banks from the SWIFT messaging system' (Adeyemo, 2022).

For global companies, this case highlights the significance of intelligence gathering and coalition-building under crisis. These qualities are not confined to diplomats. In fact, in today's volatile world of international business, executives face many of the same uncertainties and risks as diplomats. The strategic foresight, negotiation skills, and ability to build trust across borders that define successful diplomats are precisely the qualities that can help businesses thrive in turbulent times.

1.2 Why Do Executives Need the Diplomatic Approach?

The diplomatic approach offers significant insights for businesses navigating today's environment of geopolitical risks, global market uncertainties, and supply chain disruptions. A diplomat's experience in global strategic planning, negotiation, cross-cultural communication, and crisis management can help businesses enhance adaptability and develop robust international market strategies.

If we examine the Western companies' withdrawal from the Russian market after the outbreak of the war, it becomes clear that most companies were caught unprepared and suffered tremendous financial losses. According to incomplete statistics, total losses have exceeded $107 billion, highlighting the profound impact of geopolitical conflicts on businesses. European companies, in particular, have been hit hard. A survey by the *Financial Times* found that approximately 176 major European companies lost at least €100 billion due to asset write-downs, divestments, or closures of their Russian operations (Hollinger et al., 2023).

But why did these powerful multinational corporations ignore the warning signals before the war broke out? They are supposed to have strong capacities in intelligence gathering. It remains puzzling why MNCs significantly underestimate the likelihood of war. The Biden administration and British intelligence kept reminding European allies of this risk, yet many European governments appeared not to fully grasp the seriousness of these signals. Even though they embarked on diplomatic efforts in persuading Russia not to invade, these efforts were unsuccessful. More importantly, there seems to be a lack of coordination between Western governments and their companies in responding to this acute geopolitical risk. Many firms failed to put in place a 'Plan B' and diversify supply chains in advance.

One plausible explanation for the underestimation of the likelihood of war by many European governments and companies is their slow adaptation to the so-called *Zeitenwende* – the shift in the spirit of the times. Many Europeans continued to believe that the prevailing spirit of the age remained one of economic interdependence and that international institutions and diplomacy could prevent the outbreak of war. This lack of sensitivity to changing geopolitical realities blinded many European policymakers and business executives. There appears to be a strong historical inertia that slowed Europe's strategic adjustment and war preparedness.

This mindset is deeply rooted in an overreliance on economic interdependence. In countries such as Germany and France, it was widely believed that deep trade ties with Russia would deter military aggression. The doctrine of *Wandel durch Handel* ('Change through Trade') suggested that economic cooperation would foster political stability and reduce the likelihood of conflict.

The following section presents a detailed case study of the French automobile company Renault's miserable withdrawal from Russia. It equally explores how the outcome might have been different had the company adopted a more diplomatic and geopolitically informed approach at an earlier stage. We believe that Renault's experience reflects the broader predicament faced by many Western multinational corporations and therefore carries wider lessons for international business.

Case Study: The One-Ruble Sale – Renault's Exit from Russia

Renault's departure from the Russian market illustrates how geopolitical pressure, government influence, and public scrutiny can severely impact corporate decision-making. Before the Russia–Ukraine War, Renault held a significant stake in AvtoVAZ, Russia's largest car manufacturer. However, as the war escalated, Renault faced intense public pressure, particularly from the French government, its largest shareholder with a 15% stake, and from Ukrainian President Volodymyr Zelensky, who called out the company during a speech in the French National Assembly (Reuters, 2022).

French Finance Minister Bruno Le Maire publicly emphasized in March 2022 that French companies should align their business decisions with the country's political and moral stance following Russia's invasion of Ukraine, reinforcing expectations that Renault would exit the Russian market (Le Maire, 2022). Under this mounting political and public pressure, Renault announced its withdrawal, divesting its stake in AvtoVAZ for a symbolic 1 ruble, with an option to buy it back within six years (Hollinger et al., 2022). Renault CEO Luca de Meo later acknowledged that the company had limited room to manoeuvre under intense political and reputational pressure surrounding the war, emphasizing that the decision to exit Russia was necessary to protect Renault's long-term strategic interests (Hollinger et al., 2022).

The Renault case highlights the importance of businesses adopting a diplomatic approach – balancing government relations, stakeholder expectations, and geopolitical risk assessment to avoid sudden, unplanned exits that lead to significant financial losses.

If Renault had applied a diplomatic mindset, its performance and resilience could have been markedly different:

(1) Early Warning and Scenario Planning: diplomats continuously scan political landscapes and prepare contingency plans. A diplomatic approach would have treated U.S. and U.K. intelligence warnings as actionable signals, prompting Renault to explore alternative production bases, supply chain diversification, or staged disengagement strategies before the crisis escalated.

(2) Exit Strategy with Negotiated Leverage: diplomats rarely leave the table without securing concessions. Instead of a symbolic divestment under public pressure, Renault could have negotiated in advance for more favourable terms – such as joint ventures with third countries, asset swaps, or guaranteed buy-back clauses safeguarded through EU mediation – thus reducing the scale of financial loss.

(3) Reputation Management and Strategic Communication: diplomats carefully calibrate messaging to domestic and foreign audiences. Renault could have managed public perception more proactively, framing its disengagement as part of a coordinated European response, rather than appearing reactive and cornered.

1.3 The Diplomatic Approach in Business Practice

The four diplomatic competencies discussed earlier – strategic foresight and long-term thinking, strategic communication and coalition-building, negotiation tactics, and crisis management – can be translated into concrete managerial tools for international business. Rather than simply borrowing diplomatic concepts, companies can operationalize these capabilities through specific strategic practices.

1.3.1 Strategic Foresight and Long-term Thinking

Diplomats constantly assess shifts in the global balance of power and the evolving configuration of international politics in order to position their country advantageously. For multinational corporations, this capability translates into strategic foresight – the ability to interpret geopolitical trends and anticipate structural changes in the international system.

Strategic foresight for companies typically involves three analytical steps: First, firms must develop the ability to interpret geopolitical trends and structural changes in the international system. As discussed earlier, through the concept of *Shi*, successful strategic actors align their actions with the broader direction of historical and geopolitical change. For corporations, this means understanding shifts in the global power structure, technological competition, and the changing dynamics of globalization.

Second, companies must determine their strategic positioning within this evolving environment. Firms operating globally often face competing pressures from different geopolitical blocs. The example of Apple illustrates this logic. As tensions between the United States and China intensified, Apple gradually diversified parts of its production base to India and Vietnam while continuing to invest in China. This strategy reflects a form of corporate hedging between major powers in an increasingly bipolar world.

Third, firms can operationalize strategic foresight through scenario building. Instead of assuming a stable global environment, companies should construct multiple geopolitical scenarios – such as sanctions regimes, military conflicts, or supply chain fragmentation – and test how their operations would perform under each scenario. Scenario planning allows executives to identify early warning signals and prepare contingency strategies before crises emerge.

1.3.2 Strategic Communication and Socialization

Diplomatic practice emphasizes not only formal negotiations but also continuous interpersonal engagement among professionals who operate within an international community of diplomats. As illustrated by the establishment of the U.S.–China Strategic Economic Dialogue (SED), sustained personal interaction and trust between negotiators often create the conditions that make formal agreements possible.

For multinational corporations, this diplomatic logic translates into the strategic cultivation of relationship networks. Companies operating across borders must ensure that, when political tensions arise, they are able to reach the right decision-makers and communicate effectively with them. In many geopolitical situations, formal corporate channels alone are insufficient. Informal relationships with government officials, regulators, industry leaders, and local partners can become decisive in resolving crises or advancing negotiations.

Firms can operationalize this capability by investing in relationship diplomacy – maintaining regular dialogue with key stakeholders, building personal rapport with policymakers, and developing cross-cultural empathy in international teams. Rather than approaching governments only during moments of crisis, successful multinational corporations cultivate long-term interpersonal connections that allow them to communicate directly and effectively when critical decisions must be made. In this sense, strategic communication in international business is less about public messaging and more about maintaining trusted personal channels of interaction, similar to the networks diplomats rely on to defuse tensions and facilitate cooperation.

1.3.3 Negotiation across Two-Level Games

Diplomatic negotiations rarely take place on a single table. As Robert Putnam famously argued, diplomacy operates as a 'two-level game', in which negotiators must simultaneously manage bargaining at the international level while securing acceptance from domestic political actors (Putnam, 1988). Successful diplomats, therefore, navigate two interconnected arenas: negotiations with foreign counterparts abroad and negotiations with political constituencies at home.

Multinational corporations face a similar dual structure when operating in international markets. On one level, companies negotiate with host governments, regulators, partners, and competitors in foreign markets. On another level, they must respond to pressures from their home governments, shareholders, public opinion, and political institutions. Corporate decisions in international business, therefore, often emerge from the interaction between these two arenas.

As discussed earlier in the Renault case, corporate decisions in international markets are often constrained by domestic political pressures. Renault's withdrawal from Russia was shaped not only by business considerations but also by intense pressure from the French government and public opinion following the invasion of Ukraine. The episode illustrates how multinational corporations can become trapped between the two arenas of negotiation.

To operate effectively within this dual structure, companies can adopt several practical tools. Firms should conduct domestic political risk mapping, identifying the key political actors and public narratives that may influence corporate decisions at home. They should also integrate political scenario planning into negotiation strategies, anticipating how domestic reactions might constrain or reshape international bargaining outcomes.

1.3.4 Crisis Management and Strategic Intelligence

Crisis management represents one of the most demanding aspects of diplomatic practice. Diplomats operate in environments characterized by uncertainty, geopolitical tensions, and the constant possibility of conflict. As a result, they develop professional instincts for anticipating crises and responding to them under pressure. Multinational corporations, however, often lack such capabilities and therefore tend to be less prepared when geopolitical crises occur.

One structural reason lies in the asymmetry of intelligence capabilities between states and corporations. Governments possess extensive diplomatic and intelligence networks, including foreign ministries, intelligence agencies, and embassies across the world. These institutions continuously collect political, military, and economic information. Corporations, by contrast, rarely have access to such comprehensive intelligence systems. Their information sources are often fragmented and market-oriented, making it difficult to assess geopolitical risks accurately.

The experience of Western companies during the Russia–Ukraine War illustrates this challenge. Although U.S. and British intelligence had repeatedly warned of a potential Russian invasion months in advance, many companies either lacked access to such intelligence or underestimated its credibility. As a result, when the war broke out, numerous firms were forced into abrupt withdrawals from the Russian market, suffering significant financial losses.

Another factor lies in organizational culture. Diplomats and military professionals operate in environments where crises are expected and even routine. They develop the ability to remain calm under pressure and to interpret crises as dynamic processes rather than sudden catastrophes. In contrast, corporations typically operate in relatively stable market environments. When geopolitical shocks occur, financial markets and corporate decision-making structures often react abruptly and defensively.

In strategic thinking – particularly in Chinese philosophy – crises are often understood as containing both danger and opportunity. The Chinese term for crisis, *weiji* (危机), combines the characters for danger (*wei*) and opportunity (*ji*), reflecting the idea that crises may create opportunities for strategic transformation. For corporations, developing the capacity to transform risk into opportunity requires analytical discipline and institutional preparedness.

One practical tool is scenario building. Companies should systematically construct alternative geopolitical scenarios – such as sanctions regimes, armed conflicts, or technological decoupling – and assess how these scenarios would affect their operations. Historical examples demonstrate the importance of such foresight. During the 1967 Six-Day War in the Middle East, most firms expected a prolonged conflict and prepared accordingly, while a few companies correctly anticipated a rapid Israeli victory and adjusted their strategies. These firms benefited from more sophisticated geopolitical analysis and access to individuals with military or diplomatic expertise.

Ultimately, effective crisis management requires organizational capacity. Just as governments maintain strategic planning units and military staff structures, multinational corporations increasingly need dedicated strategic intelligence and geopolitical analysis teams. Such units function as the corporate equivalent of a diplomatic or military staff, responsible for monitoring geopolitical developments, assessing strategic risks, and advising senior leadership on long-term strategy.

This point is vividly illustrated in popular culture as well. In the Japanese television series *Fumō Chitai* (*The Wasteland*), the protagonist Iki Tadashi, a former Imperial Japanese Army staff officer, later becomes a senior executive in a trading company. His background as a military strategist allows him to analyse geopolitical developments and military conflicts with far greater accuracy than most corporate executives. As a result, the company gains a strategic advantage in navigating international crises and political uncertainties.

Although fictional, the story captures an important reality: corporations increasingly need individuals with strategic and geopolitical expertise – often former diplomats, military officers, or intelligence professionals – who can serve as the company's 'strategic staff'. These individuals help firms interpret geopolitical signals, assess the trajectory of conflicts, and advise senior leadership on how to respond to rapidly evolving international situations.

Below is a summary of the application of the diplomatic approach in business practice (see Table 1.2). The four diplomatic competencies discussed in this chapter – strategic foresight, relationship diplomacy, two-level negotiation, and strategic crisis intelligence – constitute the core capabilities of business diplomacy.

Table 1.2 The Business Diplomacy Framework: Applying the Diplomatic Approach in Business Practice

Diplomatic Approach	*Business Parallel and Case Study*	*Practical Tool for Executives*
Strategic foresight and long-term thinking (Shi, trend recognition, understanding structural change)	Apple supply chain diversification under U.S.–China geopolitical tensions	*Scenario Planning Matrix* – develop geopolitical scenarios and identify early warning indicators
Strategic communication and socialization (trust-building, empathy, informal diplomacy)	U.S.–China Strategic Economic Dialogue (SED) – trust built through personal diplomacy	*Relationship Network Mapping* – cultivate long-term personal connections with government and elite stakeholders
Negotiation across two-level games (Putnam's domestic–international bargaining)	Renault's exit from Russia – domestic political pressure reshaping corporate decisions	*Two-Level Negotiation Framework* – integrate domestic political risk analysis into international negotiations
Crisis management and strategic intelligence (anticipating shocks and adapting under pressure)	Western corporate withdrawal from Russia after the Ukraine War	*Corporate Strategic Intelligence Unit* – institutionalize geopolitical analysis and crisis simulations

References

Adeyemo, W. (2022). America's new sanctions strategy. *Foreign Affairs, 101*(5), 30–36.

Clinton, H. R. (2011, October 14). *Remarks to the economic club of New York*. U.S. Department of State. https://web.archive.org/web/20111105205610/http://www.state.gov/secretary/rm/2011/10/175552.htm

Flint, C., & Taylor, P. J. (2018). *Political geography: World-economy, nation-state and locality* (7th ed.). Routledge.

Hollinger, P., Sugiura, E., & Telling, O. (2023, August 6). European companies suffer 100bn hit from Russian operations since full-scale invasion of Ukraine. *Financial Times*. https://www.ft.com/content/c4ea72b4-4b02-4ee9-b34c-0fac4a4033f5

Le Maire, B. (2022, March 7). *Interview on sanctions against Russia following its invasion of Ukraine*. BFM TV/French Ministry of Economy. https://www.vie-publique.fr/discours/284274-bruno-le-maire-07032022-russie

Ministry of Foreign Affairs of the People's Republic of China. (2009, July 20). *Hu Jintao attends the 11th conference of Chinese diplomatic envoys stationed abroad and delivers an important speech*. https://www.fmprc.gov.cn/web/wjdt_674879/gjldrhd_674881/200907/t20090721_7699062.shtml

Okano-Heijmans, M. (2013). *Economic diplomacy: Japan and the balance of national interests*. Leiden and Boston: Martinus Nijhof Publishers.

Paulson, H. M. (2015). *Dealing with China: An insider unmasks the new economic superpower* (pp. 210–230). Grand Central Publishing.

Putnam, R. D. (1988). Diplomacy and domestic politics: The logic of two-level games. *International Organization, 42*(3), 427–460.

Reuters. (2022, March 23). *Zelenskiy urges French firms including Renault to leave Russia*. Reuters.

Reuters. (2023, May 15). *Apple expands production in India and Vietnam as it diversifies beyond China*. Reuters. https://www.reuters.com/

Reuters. (2024, March 24). *China told it faces 'fork in the road' as officials meet CEOs*. https://www.reuters.com/world/china/china-told-it-faces-fork-road-officials-meet-ceos-2024-03-24/

Riordan, S. (2018). *The geopolitics of cyberspace: A diplomatic perspective*. Brill.

Rogowsky, R. A. (2026). Strategic export controls and the G7 coordination challenge. *Economic Diplomacy, 4*(S1), 11–23. https://doi.org/10.2478/ecdip-2026-0002

State-owned Assets Supervision and Administration Commission of China. (2011, May 19). *Xie Hui: Reflections on frontline participation in the large-scale evacuation operation in Libya*. http://www.sasac.gov.cn/n4470048/n9369363/n9388852/n9389658/c9403635/content.html

Tzu, S. (1963). *The art of war* (S. B. Griffith, Trans.). Oxford University Press.

White House. (2014, November 10). *Fact sheet: Supporting American job growth and strengthening ties with China through extended visa validity*. The White House.

Zhang, X. (2023). *Linkage power Europe: The EU's trade negotiations with China (1975–2019)*. Routledge.

Zhang, X. (2024). *New economic statecraft: China, the United States and the European Union*. Routledge.

Zhang, X., & Flint, C. (2021). Why and whither the US-China trade war?: Not realist 'Traps' but political geography 'Capture' as explanation. *Journal of World Trade, 55*(2), 335–358.

Zhu, L. (2010). *China's foreign policy debates*. European Union Institute for Security Studies.

2 The Diplomatic Approach to Strategy

The author recently bought a book on business strategy at an airport. As a former diplomat, he was curious to learn more of the strategy tools used by business executives and taught in business schools. The book consisted of a series of such tools. What was striking was the extent to which these tools were focused on the internal structures and organization of the company. To the extent that some of the tools were applied to outside factors, these were limited to suppliers, customers, or rival competitors. These 'external stakeholders' were assumed to act rationally in the pursuit of their interests. There was no mention of the wider economic or geopolitical climate. Change seemed to be limited to new technologies, new tastes or fashions among consumers, and new market structures. There seemed to be a broad assumption of stability and predictability in the wider environment in which the company was operating. The strategy tools on offer seemed mechanistic and designed for a linear world in which the scale of outcomes can be accurately calculated from the scale of inputs. To some extent, this lack of concern with the wider world is understandable. This was a book produced towards the end of what is now called the 'Great Convergence', the period from the collapse of the Soviet Union to roughly 2003, when the United States was geopolitically dominant, and the world seemed to be converging on certain economic, if not political, principles. Although this period was less economically and financially stable than the rosy hue of hindsight allows, it was a period in which executives could focus on the organization of their own companies and the relations with their customers and competitors without too much concern for the wider context. But as we have seen, the 'Great Convergence' proved to be a false dawn. A combination of factors, including the Iraq War, the 2008 financial crisis, the rise of China, and the Russian invasion of Ukraine, has generated a far more unpredictable and unstable geopolitical environment. Business executives now ignore this wider geopolitical environment at their peril.

To be fair, business executives and business school professors have recognized the change in the international environment. The better business schools put an ever greater emphasis on courses on geopolitics. Managing uncertainty plays a greater role in courses about strategic thinking. But mechanistic strategy tools are still taught and continue to play a major role in executives'

DOI: 10.4324/9781032625089-3

strategic tool boxes. Management consultancy companies wax lyrical about the challenges of managing uncertainty in a chaotic world ('chaos theory' and 'complexity' play leading roles in their promotional materials). But the modelling tools they deploy for their clients still make assumptions about perfect information and rational actors. Major corporations continue to publish strategic plans, usually looking two years ahead. These strategic plans have little to do with strategy and essentially set out the corporation's aspirations in the hope that they will convince financial market analysts. Their relationship to future outcomes is about as meaningful as the five-year plans, so beloved to Soviet planners (and increasingly Brussels bureaucrats). The volatile economic and geopolitical environments of the 21st century make planning even two years ahead a risky enterprise. It may seem that either business executives know that these strategic plans are meaningless but promulgate them anyway, or they have not yet appreciated how much the international environment has changed over the last decade. There is a third possibility: that business executives, and management consultants, know how much the world has changed; they know how uncertain outcomes and forecasts have become over even two years; but they do not know how to deal with it. They continue to use the tools that they have. They adopt a fatalistic approach to the wider geopolitical and economic environments. If such environments are so uncertain and unpredictable, then they are beyond the control and analytic capabilities of companies and their executives. However, such fatalism is not justified. Diplomats, and soldiers, have long had to manage uncertainty and incomplete information. Strategy was their way of managing uncertainty while maintaining at least some coherence of policy. This chapter will look at the diplomatic and military approach to strategy and consider what companies and business executives can learn from it.

There has been a greater appreciation of the impact of major shocks on the international business environment since 2001, in part driven by the events of 9/11. The Scottish philosopher David Hume (1748) coined the term 'Black Swans' in the 18th century to underline the weakness of inductive reasoning. In Hume's example, all swans that had been seen in Europe had been white. Therefore, all swans were white. But when Europeans ventured to Australia, they discovered Black Swans. Did that mean that all swans were not white, or that what they had discovered in Australia were not swans? Hume's point was that inductive reasoning is always vulnerable to being disproved by the next piece of evidence. At the beginning of the millennium, Lebanese financial analyst Nassim Taleb (2007) adopted the term 'Black Swan' to mean an event with a big impact which could not have been predicted in advance. He recognized that in highly complex adaptive systems, like financial markets, human societies and the international system frequently suffer unexpected and unpredictable shocks. In such non-linear systems, small inputs can generate disproportionately large outcomes, whereas large inputs can sink without trace. Taleb (2012) argued that, as a consequence, developing resilience to shocks, what he called 'anti-fragility', was more important than efforts to predict the future. Unfortunately, the concept of 'Black Swan' was seized on by some to avoid responsibility for policy mistakes. Thus, some policymakers argued that COVID-19 was a Black Swan that could not have been anticipated. Their inability to manage the pandemic was therefore not their fault, as they were taken by surprise by an unpredictable event. Taleb himself has stated that a global pandemic was not a Black Swan as not only could such a pandemic be predicted but also much work had been done on the likelihood and likely impact of pandemics. This in turn led to the idea of 'Grey Swans' – events which were predictable but unexpected. There could be considerable knowledge of the likelihood of the event but not of its timing or precise nature. Thus, when the Grey Swan occurred, it was unexpected by observers. Stock market collapses might be considered 'Grey Swans'. The conditions which led to the financial crisis in 2008 – subprime mortgages, excessive securitization of debt, insurance of debt separated from the debt itself – were not unknown. But the timing and impact of the crisis took even seasoned observers by surprise.

The confusion between 'Black Swans' and 'Grey Swans' has led to the development of the idea of 'Dragon Kings' (Sornette, 2009). 'Dragon Kings' are events that are not unpredictable in themselves, but their scale and impact are unpredictable. This picks up on the non-linear nature of complex adaptive systems noted above. Within complex adaptive systems (Mitchell, 2009), large numbers of agents and factors interact in unpredictable ways. The interaction of positive feedback loops (exaggerating impacts) and negative feedback loops (reducing impacts) generates the non-linearity by which small events can have major impacts, whereas major events have minimal impact. In terms of former Defence Secretary Rumsfeld's famous classification, Black Swans are unknown unknowns, and Dragon Kings are known unknowns – we know they can happen, but we cannot anticipate their consequences. Prior to 1914, there were two major Balkan wars whose impact was confined to the region. The assassination of Franz Ferdinand and his wife in Sarajevo on 28 June 1914 was an apparently lesser event that developed into the Dragon King of the First World War. The scale and impact of events in complex adaptive systems follow a power law distribution: most events are small scale, but major events (Dragon Kings) do happen, just not very often. The problem with power law distributions (Clauset et al., 2009) is that they can give good descriptions of the data (e.g. the percentage of the population killed in wars) but have no predictive value (Mandelbrot & Hudson, 2004). Financial market analysts have sought to get round this by ignoring the power law nature of risk in complex adaptive systems and building their forecasting models on the basis of a normal distribution (the famous Bell-shaped distribution). Such a distribution is great for human heights and works most of the time in financial markets, but it leads analysts to underestimate the risk of major events which fall outside the normal distribution. During the 1990s, the hedge fund Long-Term Capital Management (LTCM) relied on the Scholes-Black model for options pricing, a model essentially built around a normal distribution. The model underestimated the likelihood of outlier events, like the Russian

Financial Crisis in 1998, which brought down LTCM and nearly brought down the global financial system with it. Fortunately, soldiers and diplomats during the Cold War had a better understanding of risk. They knew that, however unlikely, a major global conflagration, fuelled by nuclear weapons, was possible and worked assiduously to avoid it (Box 2.2).

Box 2.1 Case Study 1: Shell and the Oil Shock of 1973

Scenario Planning as Strategic Resilience

In the early 1970s, Royal Dutch Shell pioneered the use of scenario planning – not to forecast the future but to explore how the global oil market might evolve under varying political and economic conditions. One scenario, considered unlikely at the time, involved Arab producers restricting oil exports to the West. When the Yom Kippur War triggered exactly that in 1973, Shell had already gamed out such a situation and was able to adapt faster than its competitors.

While other oil majors scrambled to respond, Shell's internal preparedness allowed it to reallocate resources, adjust logistics, and manage stakeholder expectations more effectively. This episode exemplifies the strategic value of scenario building not as predictive prophecy but as a method of enhancing organizational resilience through the disciplined exploration of uncertainty.

Box 2.2 Case Study 2: LTCM and the Myth of Rational Markets

Non-linearity and the Limits of Financial Modelling

LTCM, a hedge fund staffed by Nobel laureates and Wall Street veterans, used sophisticated models which assumed that financial markets behaved according to a normal distribution. These models underestimated the likelihood of extreme events and over-relied on the rationality of market actors.

When Russia defaulted on its debt in 1998, markets reacted in highly correlated and unpredictable ways. LTCM's enormous leveraged positions quickly collapsed, threatening systemic contagion. The U.S. Federal Reserve had to intervene to coordinate a rescue. The crisis showed how strategies based on false certainty and linear models can collapse catastrophically when applied to complex adaptive systems. It was a stark reminder that strategy, like diplomacy, must be flexible and prepared for the improbable (Lowenstien, 2001).

Following the COVID-19 pandemic, the Russian invasion of Ukraine, and the consequent cost of living crisis, two new words entered the Western vocabulary: 'policrisis' (Tooze, 2022) and 'permacrisis'. Policrisis sought to capture the idea that policymakers, and business executives, had to face multiple crises at the same time. At the time, it was felt that the legacy of COVID-19, the Russian invasion of Ukraine, climate change, price inflation (especially energy prices), and the U.S. confrontation with China were testing the resilience of Western policymakers and their ability to manage multiple crisis at the same time (in Lyndon Baynes Johnson's memorable phrase, their ability to chew gum and walk at the same time). The situation does not appear to get any easier. The cost of living crisis may have eased, but the war in Ukraine continues as does the U.S. confrontation with China, which looks like becoming a broader Western confrontation with China. A new Middle East crisis has emerged in Gaza and Israel with the potential to expand into a wider regional conflict drawing in Iran and Hizballah. The bandwidth of policymakers is stretched, with Israel/Gaza distracting attention from Ukraine and climate change all but forgotten. If policrisis describes the horizontal axis of multiple crises at the same time, 'permacrisis' describes the temporal axis where one crisis seems to follow another in an endless stream. The financial crisis is followed by the sovereign debt crisis, which is followed by the COVID-19 pandemic, which is followed by the Russian invasions of Ukraine, and so on. In permacrisis, crisis becomes the new normal. Although the terms are new, the experiences they describe are long-standing and would have been immediately recognized by our ancestors, although with considerably less surprise than these terms seem to imply. A brief look at the 19th century reveals a series of financial and economic crises, pandemic diseases, wars, and diplomatic crises. The same could be said of any previous century, and indeed of much of the 20th century. Geoffrey Parker (2013) has shown how, in the 17th century, a combination of pandemic disease, climate change, revolution, and warfare reduced the global human population by some 30%. Historically speaking, the period of relative economic and geopolitical stability between 1991 and 2003 was the anomaly.

The permacrisis, in particular, has implications for both government and business. There is a tendency among both policymakers and business executives to treat crises as interruptions of the normal (Box 2.3). The crisis will pass sooner or later, and normality will be resumed. If the crisis is thus seen as a state of exception, extraordinary measures can be adopted to manage it, confident that the negative effects of these measures can be remedied once normalcy returns. Governments can increase spending and cut taxes, driving up fiscal deficits and sovereign debt to unsustainable levels. Central banks slash interest rates and buy assets (aka print money), recklessly increasing the money supply. Companies can increase their debts to get over difficult times while still paying out dividends to their shareholders. Companies can even borrow money to buy back their own shares to keep share prices up. The negative effects of all of these actions can be sorted out once things get back to 'normal'. But what if crisis is the new normal, with one crisis following another and no opportunity to remedy the negative effects. This is the world of permacrisis. Governments are confronted by unsustainable sovereign debt, central banks with inflated balance sheets, and companies risk becoming zombies as they struggle to service their debts. Our current approach to crisis management, whereby crisis is seen as the state of exception between periods of normalcy, has another effect. During periods of crisis, longer-term objectives can be sacrificed to the short-term requirements of crisis management. Again the promise is that the longer-term objectives will be reinstated once normalcy returns. During the energy price crisis following the Russian invasion of Ukraine, Germany reverted to coal production to meet its energy needs, abandoning its climate change targets (Box 2.4). As new crises emerge, there seems little prospect of Germany being able to return to its climate change priorities. Nineteenth-century statesmen did better. Conscious that another crisis was always around the corner, they managed to handle the crisis while maintaining longer-term objectives in sight. They were not so easily blown off course by every crisis that struck. The ability to adapt to events while maintaining the longer term course is what soldiers and diplomats call strategy.

Box 2.3 Case Study 3: Ryanair and COVID-19

Cash Reserves as a Strategic Asset

Most airlines entered the COVID-19 crisis with highly efficient but financially fragile models – low cash reserves and high reliance on debt. In contrast, Ryanair had built up substantial cash reserves before the pandemic struck. While competitors laid off staff, grounded aircraft, and sought government bailouts, Ryanair retained its workforce and continued limited operations.

This allowed Ryanair to scale up rapidly once demand returned. Its aircraft remained operational, and its pilots retained certifications, enabling a swift rebound while competitors struggled to recover. The episode illustrates the strategic value of resilience over efficiency in a permacrisis environment. In a world of successive shocks, cash is not idle – it is optionality.

Diplomats and soldiers are used, or at least were used, to taking decisions in conditions of considerable uncertainty and with insufficient information. Henry Kissinger once commented that the tragedy of foreign policy was that when you had the greatest freedom of action, you had the least information. As information increased, the freedom of action reduced (he also said that the other tragedy of foreign policy was that all the options are bad ones: the art of statecraft was guiding events towards the least bad outcome). In other words, waiting for all the information to come in before making a decision is not an option in foreign policy. By the time all the information has been gathered, other actors will have taken the decision for you. You will be left with limited, if any, options. The reader may object that this may have been true in the past, but with all the information available through the internet and other digital technologies, combined with the analytical strengths of artificial intelligence, foreign policymakers have never been better informed. They no longer have to make decisions under conditions of limited information. Uncertainty should be shrinking rather than increasing. And yet digital technologies do not really change the calculus. If anything, they make the uncertainty greater. We must distinguish between data and information. Information is data which informs our decision-making, which reduces the uncertainty around our decisions. We are drowning in data. But most of that data is unreliable or irrelevant to the decisions we must make. Identifying that key information that will reduce the uncertainty surrounding our decisions is difficult and time consuming. If we are drowning in data, we are also drowning in disinformation. The key information – for example about the motivations driving the decisions of other actors – may simply be unavailable however much technology we throw at it.

Box 2.4 Case Study 4: Germany's Energy U-Turn

Crisis Management versus Strategic Coherence

Germany, long reliant on Russian gas and committed to phasing out coal and nuclear energy, faced a brutal energy crisis following Russia's invasion of Ukraine in 2022. In response, it restarted coal-fired power plants and delayed climate initiatives to manage short-term supply shocks and price surges (International Energy Agency, 2023).

This policy reversal highlighted the fragility of strategies which assume geopolitical and economic stability. Treating the crisis as a temporary exception, rather than a symptom of deeper structural vulnerabilities, led to short-term fixes at the expense of long-term goals. In a permacrisis world, strategic planning must allow for adaptive responses without abandoning broader policy objectives. Strategy, as diplomats know, must bend without breaking.

Artificial Intelligence may not be the answer, although foreign ministries, like major corporations, are devoting much thought as to how to make use of it. The kind of AI that we are using at present has strengths and weaknesses. It is very good at identifying patterns in data, but less good at distinguishing between correlation and causation, especially where historical series of data are inconsistent (the distinction between early diagnosis of cancer, e.g., and identifying causal relationships in international events). Large Language Models (LLM), like Chat GPT, depend on developments in computing power and access to data. Neural networks are trained on enormous language data sets to enable them to predict text in response to our prompts. There are two problems with this kind of programme from the point of view of decision-makers. This is not really 'artificial intelligence' as computational statistics. The programme can have no 'understanding' of the text it generates and therefore cannot 'explain' its results. The programme must remain a black box to its users (and to some extent to the computer scientists who create it). This limits its value in decision-making processes where explanation is critical. A policymaker will not simply accept the analyst's conclusions but want to ask the inevitable 'why do you think this?'. Current AI based on neural networks and mass data finds such questions challenging. Furthermore, the reliability of the text generated depends not only on the computing power of the neural networks but also on the quality of the data on which they are trained. Any biases or prejudices in the training data will be replicated in the output of the LLM. There is no clear evidence on to what extent the creators of LLMs seek to avoid bias or prejudice in the training data. Given that the vast majority of English language text on the internet (remember that much of the text is historical – Shakespeare is internet data) was created by one group of people – white, middle-class men – avoiding bias in the training data would be a heroic task.

Artificial Intelligence therefore, for now at least, offers no clear and reliable way for foreign policymakers, in government or the private sector, to sift through the data that constantly bombards to find the key information that can inform their decisions. Taking decisions in conditions of uncertainty and imperfect information remains the fate of the diplomat. And she knows, as Kissinger pointed out, that she cannot wait for ever more information to flow in, in the hope that it may make things clearer. The longer she waits the fewer options she has, the less chance she has to influence events. This was illustrated by the differing approaches to COVID-19 by Asian and European governments. Asian governments very quickly treated the outbreak of COVID-19 as a national security issue (possibly because of their previous experience with SARS). They understood that if they waited for information to accrue, their freedom of action would be limited. They acted immediately to limit the disease's spread. European governments instead saw COVID-19 as a public health issue. There has been a growth in recent years of the idea of evidence-led policy – policy should be designed only after acquiring and analysing the evidence. European governments wanted to wait for the evidence before adopting measures to limit the spread of the disease. The delays proved fatal. In the end, they were left with limited options – the disease took the decisions for them – and lockdowns of varying severity were imposed in most European countries. Needless to say, the outcomes in most Asian countries were significantly better than in their European counterparts.

The Foreign Ministry official sitting in her office will be well versed in the idea of policrisis. The more senior she becomes, the greater will be her need to manage multiple crises at the same time. The way in which the number of crises she is expected to manage increase as she moves up within the ministry illustrates an important aspect of the management and mitigation of geopolitical risk: the management of such crises and the policy decisions they require depend on subjective decisions and intuition. It is not immediately clear, or even with the benefit of hindsight, if the decisions she took were correct (historians still debate furiously whether Chamberlain got Munich wrong, or what alternatives were available to him). The ability for intuitive decision-making is developed over years through experience, which often explains the mistakes made by politicians thrust into foreign policy without those years of experience. We shall return to this later in the chapter.

Our Foreign Ministry official also knows that outcomes do not depend on her decision or those of her government alone. As the military like to say, the other guy has a vote. Foreign policy is more difficult than domestic policy in the sense that adopting a policy is the start of the policy rather than the end. In domestic policy, once a government has decided on a policy, the only challenge is implementation. This can be challenging in itself, and the implementation of a policy inevitably results in a series of unforeseen consequences, which is why government often seems like an endless game of Whack-A-Mole. Despite this, the government has the full panoply of the state – police forces, courts, the civil service, etc. – to support the implementation of its policy. But in foreign policy, deciding on the policy is only the first step in a long process of negotiation with allies and rivals before the implementation of the policy becomes even a possibility. And by that point, assuming that the policy has made it that far, it is likely to look very different from the policy the government decided in the first place. In this process, not only does 'the other guy have a vote', but also the other guy may not be rational, or at least not rational in the same way as you. We have already mentioned how traditional economic and business models assume rational actors in pursuit of their own interests. There is growing recognition that this may not always be true, with concepts such as bounded rationality. But even so, these models assume that there is an objective reality on which the actors agree. In foreign policy, it is not only the calculation of interests but also the perception of reality that differ. A foreign actor may not only see his interests as different from mine but may also have a very different perception of the reality about which we are arguing.

The negotiations between China and the UK over Hong Kong provide an interesting example. In the Joint Declaration of 1984, the British government agreed to return Hong Kong to Chinese sovereignty in 1997, and the Chinese government agreed to maintain Hong Kong's economic, judicial, and administrative systems unchanged for 50 years. China interpreted the agreement in terms of the UK restoring Chinese sovereignty in exchange for maintaining its economic position in Hong Kong and receiving commercial benefits in mainland China. They assumed that Hong Kong would be handed over as it was in 1984 – a free-market economy with an authoritarian colonial government. However, British officials were more concerned about the fate of the Hong Kong people, whom they were handing over to China without consultation, than Britain's economic interests. In the negotiations following the 1984 Declaration, British diplomats sought to negotiate a series of agreements to emphasize the autonomy of Hong Kong while seeking to introduce growing elements of democracy. Chinese officials could not understand why British diplomats seemed so uninterested in Britain's economic interests and began to suspect that Britain was looking to secure de facto control of Hong Kong even after it returned to Chinese sovereignty. These suspicions dogged subsequent negotiations and wider Sino-UK relations after 1997. Both sides had very different perceptions of the negotiations and what they were trying to achieve.

An interesting implication of the permacrisis relates to the holding of cash in companies. In a stable geopolitical and economic environment, holding cash in companies is seen as inefficient. Cash should be invested, whether in new technology or production facilities or in financial instruments. As noted above, recent years have seen an increasing tendency to boost share value through share buy-back schemes, whether using company profits or borrowing from financial markets. At times of geopolitical and economic stability and low interest rates, leveraging a company to secure better returns on financial instruments can make sense. But permacrisis changes the calculations. If we are living in a permacrisis where crisis is the new normal, companies need to retain more cash to get through the successive crises. The extent to which a company is cash rich contributes to its resilience against permacrisis. Cash-poor or over-leveraged companies eventually encounter one crisis too many. The aviation industry during the COVID-19 pandemic provides an interesting example. Most airlines are traditionally cash poor. They focus on efficiency and retaining the least amount of cash necessary within the company. These airlines responded to the COVID-19 pandemic by laying off staff, radically cutting back on flights and mothballing aircraft. The exception was Ryanair, which was cash rich. This enabled it to continue operating flights and retain staff even though the flights were empty. This gave Ryanair significant advantages when the demand for air travel picked up as the pandemic weakened. Ryanair's aircraft were operational and did not need extensive maintenance to bring them to readiness. Ryanair did not need to recruit new staff, and all their staff had maintained the relevant qualifications up to date to allow them to operate. Ryanair was well placed to respond to the renewed demand for international air travel. Other airlines were not as well placed. Moth-balled aircraft required significant maintenance to make them operational again. Staff needed to be recruited to replace those laid off during the crisis. Pilots needed to renew their licences which had fallen into abeyance. Cabin crew needed training. These airlines were not able to respond successfully to the increase in demand. They suffered widespread cancellations and significant customer irritation. It is arguable that Ryanair, by being cash rich, was more resilient to the crisis than more 'efficient' airlines.

The Rashomon effect (Box 2.5) underlines the importance of diplomatic empathy, the ability of the diplomat to see the world through the eyes of the other, including the actions of his own government. The good diplomats understand that other countries and their diplomats have different culture and different perceptions of the world (Jervis, 1976). They work hard to understand those cultures and perceptions and to interpret them to their governments. Too often, especially today, their governments misinterpret this as 'going native' – as pleading the cause of the foreigner instead of fighting for their own country's interests. But this diplomatic empathy is as essential in making good foreign policy as it is in playing a game like chess. A chess player who worries only about his own moves and sticks to his plan, regardless of his opponent, will soon lose. A strong player tries to see the board through the eyes of his opponent and work out what he is trying to do. He also tries to understand how his opponent sees his own moves and what his opponent may do to thwart him. This becomes an iterative process throughout the game, with the strong chess player amending his assessment of his opponent's intentions and his own plans as the game progresses. The chess player must be able to conceive of an opponent who sees the board very differently to himself. We have acknowledged that business school approaches have gradually begun to include other actors, including a broader range of stakeholders such as suppliers and lawmakers as well as customers and competitors. But they still assume that these are actors who are rational in the same way that we are rational. We can assume that they see the world in the same way that we do and that in any given situation, they will behave in the same way that we do. In international relations, this is known as the fallacy of mirror imaging. It might work when talking about other companies within the same sector and business culture, but it is dangerous when analysing and seeking to mitigate geopolitical risk.

Box 2.5 Case Study 5: The Rashomon of Hong Kong

Misperception, Empathy, and Strategic Failure

The 1984 Sino-British Joint Declaration on Hong Kong committed both sides to preserving the city's economic and legal systems post-handover. But the two governments viewed the agreement through fundamentally different lenses. British officials, concerned about Hong Kong's population, emphasized political autonomy and democratic reform. Chinese negotiators interpreted this as a potential British effort to maintain de facto control and undermine Chinese sovereignty.

Both sides acted sincerely but with different mental maps – an instance of what has come to be called the *Rashomon effect* (Kurosawa, 1950). As with the conflicting narratives in Kurosawa's film, each side genuinely believed its interpretation, setting the stage for future tensions. The case underscores the need for diplomatic empathy: understanding how others perceive reality, especially when those perceptions diverge from our own. Strategic blindness to such differences can have lasting consequences – not only for governments but also for global companies operating across cultural and political boundaries.

In 1950, the Japanese film director Akira Kurosawa released the film *Rashomon*. The film has given its name to the Rashomon effect. In the film, a samurai and his wife encounter a bandit in the woods. The samurai is killed, and the bandit and the samurai's wife have a sexual encounter. The incident is witnessed by a woodcutter. Each of the participants, including the samurai through a medium and the woodcutter, gives their account of the events. The accounts all differ significantly. For example the bandit claims that he had consensual sex with the samurai's wife and killed the samurai in self-defence when he attacked him. The samurai's wife claims that she was raped by the bandit who killed her husband when he tried to intervene. The point is not only that each participant has his or her version of the events and that version is self-serving but also that each participant comes to sincerely believe their version. In the context of geopolitics, divergent countries can have radically different perceptions of events which are equally sincerely held. Because the 'other' does not see the situation in the same way as us does not mean that he is being dishonest or cynical. He may be as convinced of his version as we are of ours. The classic case from diplomacy is the argument about whether NATO gave Russia assurances that it would not expand into former Soviet Republics. NATO maintains that there were no written assurances, and the Russians are equally adamant that they received verbal assurances. In fact, the evidence suggests that Russia may have some justification for their belief, but that does not matter. The important point is that both sides are sincerely convinced of their version and that this influences their behaviour. It has, for example, played a significant role in the Russian invasion of Ukraine (Sarotte, 2021).

The analogy of the chess match has illustrated another aspect of strategy as practised by diplomats and soldiers. It is iterative and constantly changing. Strategy is not a document that you submit to the board of a company for approval but a practice in which you participate. It is not a rigid plan but a flexible and dynamic guide to behaviour which changes as the world changes. As in the chess game, our moves and the moves of other actors change the realities we have to deal with, and this must be constantly taken into account in our strategic thinking. Strategy is auto-reflexive: it changes the world and in turn is changed by the world. This reinforces the absurdity of the two-year strategic plans so beloved of company boards. They might serve their purpose in winning over market analysts, but if the company executives regard them as a fixed blueprint for corporate decisions over the next two years, they are likely to result in disaster. This is all the more so when political and geopolitical risks and opportunities have to be factored in as well as commercial and economic ones. This does not mean that diplomats do not plan at all, but rather that they regard it as a continuous process rather than an activity leading to a fixed plan. President Eisenhower (1957), thinking back to his time as the supreme commander of allied forces in Europe, once commented that the plan was nothing, but that planning was everything. What he meant was that the planning process was valuable in itself. Reality would soon overtake the plan, but the planning process left you better able to adapt to the changing environment and the unpleasant surprises the world had in store for you. As Eisenhower added, 'the very definition of emergency is that it is unexpected; therefore, it is not going to happen the way you are planning'. The activity of planning enables us better to understand the range of possible futures as well as our own vulnerabilities.

Von Moltke was a 19th-century field marshal credited with Prussian success in the so-called unification wars which enabled Bismarck to unify the German empire in 1870. He famously said that no plan survives first contact with the enemy. Actually, he said, 'The tactical result of an engagement forms the base for new strategic decisions because victory or defeat in battle changes the situation to such a degree that no human acumen is able to see beyond the first battle'. In this sense one should understand Napoleon's saying, 'I have never had a plan of operations'. Therefore, no plan of operations extends with any certainty beyond the first contact with the main hostile force'. Mike Tyson was pithier: 'everyone has a plan until I punch them in the mouth'. For Von Moltke, strategy was a system of expedients. More than a merely scholarly discipline, it was the translation of knowledge to practical life, the improvement of the original leading thought in accordance with continually changing situations. For diplomats, strategy is a continuous process which enables them to adapt to the inevitable emergencies and challenges that the world throws up without being forced to abandon their more general policy objectives. The challenge of the permacrisis is how to deal with successive major crises in which crisis becomes the new normal without being distracted or diverted from overall long-term objectives. Strategy, in the diplomatic or military sense of being an activity or process, is the answer (Von Moltke, 1993).

The question remains of how companies can effectively think strategically in analysing and mitigating geopolitical risks in their operating environment (Kahneman & Tversky, 1979). Various techniques and tools have been developed. Probably best known is scenario building, largely developed by Shell in the 1950s and since widely adopted by governments and other companies. Scenario building does not seek to forecast the future. Rather, it seeks to tell a series of stories which enable us to explore future possibility spaces. Scenario-building exercises will seek to identify the factors impacting the futures we are interested in (in other words, what areas of human activity – they could be sectoral or geographic). They then try to identify the drivers which will decide how the factors will develop. On this basis, the scenarios themselves can be developed, usually four or five. The scenarios should be plausible, there should be a clear path from the present to the scenario, and they should be interesting and help us explore something we are interested in. Increasingly individual scenarios are given titles which draw attention while saying something about the scenario (Box 2.1). A good scenario exercise allows us to ask 'what if' questions, exploring the strengths and vulnerabilities of a government or a company in possible futures. Those futures can be 5 or 15 years into the future, depending on the questions that interest us. By exploring a range of possible futures through scenario building, we better understand the future that actually happens and how to react to it. As with planning, to some extent, it is the scenario-building exercise rather than the scenarios themselves which is valuable, as it gives a better understanding of the factors and drivers shaping our futures as a government or company. The most famous example of the use of scenarios by a company was by Shell in the 1960s when they did an exercise on the future of the oil industry. They were not trying to predict the future but rather explore possible futures. One of the scenarios focused on Arab countries, restricting their sale of oil to Western oil companies. Although Shell did not expect it to happen, when the Arab countries imposed the oil embargo following the Yom Kippur war in 1973, Shell was better placed than other oil companies to know how to respond. There is a caveat: just as scenario building should not be used to predict the future, so there should be no favourite scenarios which are thought more likely. In a scenario-building exercise, all scenarios must be held to be equally probable (Schwartz, 1991). Scenario-building exercises can help develop effective strategy by allowing us to explore the possible challenges that our strategies may have to deal with and in helping explore the thinking of competitors or geopolitical actors who may affect our outcomes. When done well, they help to open the strategist's mind to possibilities that might otherwise not have occurred to her. There are other techniques which can also do this. Simulation exercises can be designed to explore in more detail different individual scenarios, allowing diplomats or executives to play the roles of different actors trying to get into 'their minds' (the diplomatic empathy we discussed above). Red teaming arose during the Cold War, when in NATO wargames, NATO forces were the blue team and Soviet forces were the red team. The idea of the exercises was to test NATO military planning. Over time, the red teamers came to enjoy testing to destruction their colleagues best-laid plans. Red teaming has progressively moved out of the military context to allow diplomatic and commercial strategies to be tested to identify weaknesses and vulnerabilities (in a cyber version, penetration, or pen testing, is used to test an organization's cybersecurity). All of these techniques help identify an organization's weaknesses and vulnerabilities and reinforce its ability to build resilience in a geopolitically vulnerable world.

As we have suggested, the requirements for long-term success, and even survival, in the world of permacrisis and policrisis are very different from those that dominated in the previous 'normality'. Being cash rich may make no sense in a stable business environment, but in an economically and geopolitically volatile environment, it may be a sensible precaution, especially as governments and central banks increasingly find themselves without fiscal or monetary tools in their armoury. In a hostile and volatile world, resilience takes priority over short-term profits or shareholder value. We will look at networking and coalition-building in a separate chapter, but it may require a different approach to competitors. Companies competing in given sectors face similar geopolitical risks and challenges which are best met through cooperation and forming alliances. Commercial competitors may become geopolitical partners, an idea that would come as no surprise to diplomats who will cooperate with a given country in one area while competing with it in another. Chinese EV companies are confronting tariffs imposed by a European Commission eager to protect European EV makers and prevent the market being overwhelmed by cheaper Chinese products. The challenges this poses to Chinese EV makers are common across the sector. Chinese EV makers would do best to collaborate in developing common strategies to meet these challenges rather than competing for any market share that may be left.

We have already suggested that the ability to take decisions in conditions of uncertainty and limited information, and to think strategically, depends as much on subjective judgement, intuition, and imagination as it does on rational analysis. These are not learnt in the lecture hall or from reading textbooks but through experience and practice (an interesting study of decision-making among fire crew found that intuition is a codeword for experience). The military have always understood this, and wargames and simulations have always played a key role in training young officers (real wars are usually too infrequent and a rather extreme approach for training officers to take decisions). Diplomatic academies also increasingly use such practical exercises to train young diplomats. Digital and virtual reality (VR) platforms are being developed to facilitate such practical training online (always an advantage when your diplomats are scattered around the world). The private sector should take advantage of these developments in training their executives. In the world of permacrisis and policrisis, business executives also need to acquire the ability to take decisions in conditions of uncertainty and imperfect information and to think strategically. Shortcuts to the practical experience which secures this ability need to be taken advantage of.

References

Clauset, A., Shalizi, C. R., & Newman, M. E. J. (2009). Power-law distributions in empirical data. *SIAM Review, 51*(4), 661–703.

Eisenhower, D. D. (1957, November 14). *Remarks at the National Defense Executive Reserve Conference* [Speech]. The White House.

Hume, D. (1748). *An enquiry concerning human understanding*. A. Millar.

International Energy Agency. (2023). *Energy policy review: Germany 2023*. https://www.iea.org/reports/germany-2023

Jervis, R. (1976). *Perception and misperception in international politics*. Princeton University Press.

Kahneman, D., & Tversky, A. (1979). Prospect theory: An analysis of decision under risk. *Econometrica, 47*(2), 263–291.

Kurosawa, A. (Director). (1950). *Rashōmon* [Film]. Daiei Film.

Lowenstein, R. (2001). *When genius failed: The rise and fall of long term capital management*. Random House.

Mandelbrot, B. B., & Hudson, R. L. (2004). *The (mis)behavior of markets: A fractal view of risk, ruin, and reward*. Basic Books.

Mitchell, M. (2009). *Complexity: A guided tour*. Oxford University Press.

Parker, G. (2013). *Global crisis: War, climate change and catastrophe in the seventeenth century*. Yale University Press.

Sarotte, M. E. (2021). *Not one inch: America, Russia, and the making of post–Cold War stalemate*. Yale University Press.

Schwartz, P. (1991). *The art of the long view: Planning for the future in an uncertain world*. Currency Doubleday.

Sornette, D. (2009). Dragon-kings, black swans and the prediction of crises. *European Physical Journal Special Topics, 205*(1), 1–26.

Taleb, N. N. (2007). *The black swan: The impact of the highly improbable*. Random House.

Taleb, N. N. (2012). *Antifragile: Things that gain from disorder*. Random House.

Tooze, A. (2022, October 28). *Welcome to the world of the polycrisis*. Foreign Policy. https://foreignpolicy.com/2022/10/28/polycrisis-adam-tooze-great-power-competition-global-finance-climate/

Von Moltke, H. (1993). *Moltke on the art of war: Selected writings* (D. J. Hughes, Ed.). Presidio Press.

3 Company-Centred Analysis of Geopolitical Risk

After an online speech on geopolitics, one of the authors of this book was approached by a senior executive of a global ICT company. This executive had long been puzzled by the behaviour of his American competitor and found inspiration and possible answers in that speech. As it happened a long time ago, the author can no longer recall which specific geopolitical insights resonated with the executive. However, following that initial contact, the author was invited to provide further consultancy focused on geopolitical analysis. This experience suggests that geopolitics has been prevalent in global competition within the ICT sector. More broadly, the anecdote reflects a larger reality: companies are becoming increasingly involved in geopolitical dynamics, yet many business executives have not fully realized this shift.

Geopolitical risk has moved to the top of corporate agendas in recent years as businesses confront an era of heightened instability and uncertainty (McKinsey & Company, 2023). A string of disruptive events since 2020 – from global trade wars and a pandemic to armed conflicts – has underscored that no company is immune. As one stark warning put it: 'You may not be interested in geopolitics, but geopolitics is interested in you' (McKinsey & Company, 2023). This quote – attributed to an October 2023 Five Eyes intelligence alliance statement to business leaders – encapsulates the new reality that even companies focused on markets and supply chains must reckon with geopolitical forces beyond their control. Indeed, recent executive surveys show that CEOs and board directors now view geopolitical tension as one of the biggest risks to economic growth and business performance.

In this context, company-level geopolitical risk analysis has become a crucial facet of strategic management. Businesses operating in a fragmenting world face 'permacrisis' conditions, from sanctions to supply shocks. Traditional risk management approaches that treated geopolitics as a distant backdrop are no longer sufficient. Instead, firms are increasingly adopting *business diplomacy* – integrating geopolitical awareness and diplomatic mindsets into corporate strategy – to navigate a world where international politics and geography can directly affect the bottom line. This chapter provides an in-depth analysis of geopolitical risks at the company level, expanding on how these

DOI: 10.4324/9781032625089-4

risks differ from state-level geopolitics and how firms can identify, anticipate, and mitigate them.

3.1 Defining Geopolitical Risk

A widely cited definition states that geopolitical risks encompass risks related to wars, terrorist acts, and tensions between states that disrupt the normal and peaceful course of international relations (Caldara & Iacoviello, 2018). However, this definition remains somewhat insufficient, as it is too generic, does not clearly distinguish geopolitical risk from the broader concept of political risk, and provides little guidance on how to anticipate such risks. Understanding *geo*political risks requires an acknowledgement of their geographical foundations – only by integrating the 'geo' back into the analysis of business and political risks (Flint, 2022) can we accurately assess their origins and implications.

Building on this, we adopt a simple definition: geopolitical risk is 'an international risk provoked by geography-related acts' (Zhang & Xu, 2020). Such acts involve the exploitation, shaping, competition, or control of specific territorial spaces. The Russia–Ukraine War exemplifies this dynamic, as it has fundamentally altered territorial boundaries, reshaped regional power balances, and displaced millions of people. Another example is Iran's attempts to block and weaponize the Strait of Hormuz after the outbreak of war in the Middle East. This definition also resonates with the classic understanding of geopolitics as 'the struggle over the control of geographical entities with an international and global dimension, and the use of such geographical entities for political advantage' (Flint, 2017, p. 36).

A longer and more elaborate definition frames geopolitical risk as an international political risk – whether existing or emerging – arising from changes in geographical structures and interests driven by the strategic use of territory, borders, infrastructure, and networks by state or non-state actors (Zhang & Xu, 2020). By grounding the analysis of geopolitical risks in territorial and spatial considerations, businesses and policymakers are better equipped to anticipate and respond to emerging threats, reinforcing the role of business diplomacy in mitigating risks and enhancing resilience in an uncertain global landscape.

Geopolitical risks – once considered the exclusive domain of governments and intelligence agencies – have moved to the core of corporate decision-making. Recent events underscore how international political instability, armed conflicts, and shifting regulatory regimes can reshape global commerce almost overnight. Thousands of Western companies were compelled to exit Russia following the invasion of Ukraine, while hundreds of Chinese high-tech and state-owned enterprises have been blacklisted by U.S. authorities. Firms such as Huawei and TikTok continue to face national security investigations, forced divestments, and regulatory battles in Western markets.

To make matters worse, many companies are stuck in the U.S.–China rivalry. For instance, Didi, China's largest ride-hailing platform, faced severe regulatory punishment after its 2021 listing in the United States, as Chinese regulators argued that allowing U.S. authorities potential access to audit working papers associated with the listing could pose national security risks (Reuters, 2021a). These examples illustrate that geopolitical shocks are no longer abstract background conditions but direct threats to corporate continuity. Business diplomacy has therefore become essential for resilience, enabling firms to anticipate risks, engage governments, and safeguard operations in an increasingly volatile environment.

Yet the scope of risk extends beyond traditional geopolitics. Traditional geopolitics typically refers to interstate rivalry expressed through military power, territorial disputes, or security alliances. Today, however, competition among major powers increasingly unfolds through economic and regulatory instruments rather than through direct military confrontation. States are increasingly weaponizing trade, technology, and finance as tools of economic statecraft. The U.S. CHIPS Act and semiconductor export bans seek to contain China's technological rise; the European Union's Global Human Rights Sanctions Regime imposes penalties on companies implicated in violations abroad; and China's Anti-Foreign Sanctions Law authorizes retaliation against firms that comply with foreign restrictions. For multinational corporations, these competing regulatory systems generate a precarious balancing act, forcing companies to navigate between conflicting legal frameworks and political pressures. In this environment, business diplomacy is no longer a matter of strategic advantage but a practical necessity, providing the means to reconcile divergent national interests while minimizing exposure to economic coercion.

3.2 Categories of Geopolitical Risks for Companies

As the author was putting the final touches to this book, the war in Iran has entered its 10th day. The Strait of Hormuz was almost blocked, and the gasoline price rose to two euros per litre – a psychological threshold for many consumers. French President Emmanuel Macron ordered the French aircraft carrier *Charles de Gaule* to the eastern Mediterranean and prepared to defend the Strait of Hormuz for French economic interests. The escalation of tensions in the Middle East posed acute geopolitical threats to global companies. But how should this type of geopolitical risk be categorized? As explained above, such risks are deeply rooted in geographical factors. In this case, the key factor is the control of so-called 'chokepoints'. The disruption or control of critical chokepoints can generate severe geopolitical risks for international trade and global business operations. Therefore, in categorizing geopolitical risks, the first step is to identify the underlying drivers and structural roots that give rise to geopolitical instability. Only by identifying the drivers and roots can companies develop strategies to anticipate and mitigate such risks. In this section, we categorize geopolitical risks into three broad types: territorial geopolitical risks, strategic chokepoint risks, and geoeconomic risks.

3.2.1 Territorial Geopolitical Risks

Territorial disputes pose direct risks to companies operating in or near the contested areas. But where are these contested areas most likely to emerge? To answer this question, we offer two classic geopolitical theories: Heartland theory and Rimland theory. A good understanding of these theories can help companies anticipate geopolitical risks.

Sir Halford Mackinder (1904), a British geographer, proposed that the key to global dominance lay in controlling the Eurasian landmass, particularly what he termed the 'Heartland' – a vast region stretching from Eastern Europe to Siberia. His famous dictum states, 'Who rules East Europe commands the Heartland; who rules the Heartland commands the World-Island; who rules the World-Island commands the world'. Mackinder also described a crescent belt surrounding the Heartland that would serve to contain Russian expansion. In this framework, regions such as Central and Eastern Europe, Central Asia, and Afghanistan become strategically significant arenas of great-power competition. During the Cold War, this theory influenced containment strategies against the Soviet Union, and today, it resonates in China's Belt and Road Initiative (BRI) and the U.S.–China rivalry in Eurasia.

The strategic significance of Mackinder's Heartland becomes particularly visible when conflicts erupt in this region. The Russia–Ukraine War provides a striking example of how territorial conflict in a geopolitically sensitive region can rapidly disrupt international business operations and force multinational corporations into costly strategic decisions.

Box 3.1 Western Multinationals and the Russia–Ukraine Conflict

Perhaps the most dramatic geopolitical risk event for companies in recent memory has been the Russia–Ukraine War that erupted in February 2022. When Russia invaded Ukraine, it not only upended European security but also triggered a massive response from the United States, EU, and allied countries in the form of extensive sanctions. These sanctions, along with voluntary actions, led to an unprecedented corporate exodus from Russia.

Prior to 2022, Russia was a major market for many Western multinationals – from oil giants (BP, Shell, ExxonMobil) to carmakers (Renault, Toyota), consumer goods firms (McDonald's, Coca-Cola, Unilever), industrial manufacturers (GE, Siemens), and tech companies

(IBM, SAP). It was seen as high risk by some, but still a G20 economy with a large consumer base and rich natural resources. That changed virtually overnight. As Russian troops advanced and horrifying images of war and humanitarian crisis emerged, doing business in Russia became untenable due to both legal barriers and reputational reasons. Governments imposed sanctions on Russian banks, individuals, and certain industries; they also severely restricted exports of key technologies to Russia. Meanwhile, public opinion and shareholder pressure mounted on companies to distance themselves from Moscow's regime.

Within weeks, over a thousand foreign companies announced plans to suspend or exit operations in Russia (Marrow, 2025). Some exits were temporary suspensions hoping for peace; others became permanent sales or departures as the war dragged on. A Yale University team tracked these exits and classified firms by degree of withdrawal, illustrating the breadth of the corporate response (Sonnenfeld et al., 2022). Companies had to navigate a patchwork of Russian retaliatory measures as well – Russia passed laws threatening nationalization of assets of companies that left, and it imposed restrictions on foreign currency transfers, trapping some firms' cash. By early 2024, a Reuters analysis calculated that Western companies had incurred at least $107 billion in losses from the Russian pull-out, in the form of asset write-downs and lost revenue (Marrow, 2025). For example BP took a $25 billion charge after writing off its stake in Russian oil company Rosneft, and French carmaker Renault sold its Russian subsidiary (including the iconic Lada brand) for a token sum (reportedly 1 ruble) with a clause that they might buy it back in the future (Marrow, 2025). McDonald's, a symbol of post-Soviet globalization, closed over 800 restaurants and sold them to a local licensee (who rebranded them). Those who stayed (a minority of primarily consumer health and agriculture companies) faced criticism and a very uncertain operating environment. A few had assets seized: Danone and Carlsberg, which had signalled intent to leave, saw the Russian government temporarily take control of their local subsidiaries in mid-2023, effectively confiscating them (Marrow, 2025).

From a risk management perspective, this case was a severe test of crisis planning and values alignment. Companies that had scenario plans for a Russia–NATO confrontation likely executed them (though many admitted privately that the scale of sanctions exceeded expectations). It forced firms to make painful choices: incur huge financial hits now or risk reputational ruin and legal jeopardy by continuing business as usual. Most chose the former, indicating a shift in how companies weigh geopolitical risk – the social licence to operate mattered as much as pure profit calculations. It also showcased the importance of agility: McDonald's, for example, managed to sell and exit within a few months, having contingency plans from earlier (it had faced a less severe Russian sanctions situation in 2014 after Crimea, which might have been a warning shot).

In terms of mitigation, many companies learnt the hard way about geographic diversification. Those that had Russia as only a small part of their revenue could absorb the loss; a few that were overexposed to Russia (like Raiffeisen Bank International, which derived half its profits from Russia, or French retailer Leroy Merlin heavily present in Russia) faced far tougher predicaments. Going forward, multinationals are likely to factor in 'could we exit this market if we had to?' into their investment decisions. The war also spurred interest in political risk insurance (though many existing policies did not pay out for sanctions-related losses, as war and sanctions are often exclusions or had insufficient coverage limits for such a systemic event).

Another notable aspect was coordination and information-sharing: industry groups and consulting firms facilitated peer learning as companies figured out how to unwind operations, handle employee transitions (many had Russian staff to take care of), and comply with evolving rules. This collective action resembles how governments act in crises, showing companies acting almost as diplomatic actors – some CEOs engaged directly with government officials to get guidance or leniency on certain matters (e.g. ensuring humanitarian exceptions for food/medicine).

Nicholas Spykman (1942), an American political scientist, modified Mackinder's Heartland theory by arguing that the coastal regions (Rimland) of Eurasia – Western Europe, the Middle East, South Asia, and East Asia – were more crucial than the Heartland itself. His theory suggested that whoever controls the Rimland controls Eurasia and, thus, global power. This perspective greatly influenced U.S. Cold War strategies (such as containing the Soviet Union by forming the North Atlantic Treaty Organization (NATO), Southeast Asia Treaty Organization (SEATO), and alliances in the Middle East and East Asia).

The territorial disputes in the South China Sea are a typical example that relates to Spykman's Rimland theory. These disputes, where multiple countries dispute maritime borders, pose significant risks to oil and gas companies exploring offshore fields. Rimland theory suggests that coastal zones and maritime–continental interfaces often become geopolitically sensitive spaces. As Colin Flint (2024) argues in his analysis of *near seas*, waters that appear geographically 'near' to one state may simultaneously be viewed as strategically important 'far seas' by rival powers seeking influence. For China, the South China Sea constitutes a near sea that is closely linked to its national security and maritime strategy. For the United States, however, maintaining freedom of navigation and strategic access in these waters is essential for preserving its broader influence across the Indo-Pacific. These competing strategic interests periodically generate tensions that create risks for businesses operating in the region. Moreover, in 2014, Vietnamese–Chinese tensions flared when China placed an oil rig in contested waters, leading to anti-Chinese riots in Vietnam that targeted factories (some of which were Taiwanese or South Korean-owned, mistaken as Chinese) – foreign factories suffered damage due to a geopolitical dispute unrelated to them except by location (Vo, 2014). These cases show that territorial geopolitics can erupt suddenly, and companies caught in the middle may face evacuations, property loss, or violence.

We introduce these classic geopolitical theories to remind business executives that foreign-policy elites and military strategists often interpret global politics through such geopolitical maps. For them, the world is not merely a collection of markets but a strategic landscape defined by power competition and geographic constraints. To anticipate geopolitical risks effectively, companies must learn to interpret international developments through similar analytical lenses. In major corporate decisions – particularly those involving large fixed investments – firms benefit from having advisors who understand geopolitical strategy and who can think in ways similar to diplomats and military planners. Otherwise, companies may inadvertently become entangled in great-power rivalry and face accusations of ignoring national interests or acting against public sentiment.

3.2.2 Strategic Chokepoint Risks

Strategic chokepoints are narrow channels – geographic or logistical – through which a significant portion of global trade or resources flow. Alfred Thayer Mahan (1890), a U.S. naval officer and strategist, was among the first thinkers to systematically emphasize the strategic importance of such chokepoints in his theory of sea power. Classic examples are the Suez Canal, the Strait of Hormuz, the Strait of Malacca, the Panama Canal, or key rail corridors and pipelines. Because so much commerce funnels through these tight spaces, they are vulnerable single points of failure. Geopolitically, states recognize these chokepoints as strategic assets or liabilities; conflicts or power plays often centre on controlling or disrupting them. For companies, the risk is that a chokepoint becomes contested or closes due to geopolitical events, thereby blocking the flow of goods and crippling supply chains. Even short disruptions can have outsized effects due to the high volume of trade concentrated there. The risk is inherently geographic – it's about specific, critical locations on the world map whose status determines whether products can move from point A to B.

Firms reliant on global supply chains – especially those following just-in-time (JIT) inventory models – are extremely sensitive to chokepoint disruptions. A sudden blockage can delay shipments, cause stockouts of inputs, spike transportation costs (as ships reroute thousands of miles), and ultimately hit revenues and customer relationships. The classic illustration occurred in March 2021, when the Ever Given container ship ran aground in the Suez Canal, halting traffic for six days. Approximately 12% of global trade passes through the Suez Canal (New Zealand Ministry of Foreign Affairs and Trade, 2021), so this single accident had a worldwide impact. Economists estimated that each day of immobilization delayed $6 to $10 billion worth of goods (Allianz SE, 2021). Companies across industries – from automotive manufacturers waiting on parts to retailers awaiting shipments – scrambled as over 300 vessels backed up. Some ships detoured around Africa (adding weeks and fuel costs), while others simply waited. The incident cost large shipping companies like Maersk tens of millions in direct losses, and its ripple effects (port congestion, container shortages) lasted for months. Although the Suez blockage was not deliberately caused by political conflict, it underscored how a geographically specific event can cascade through global business.

Box 3.2 examines another major chokepoint – the Panama Canal – where geopolitical competition between the United States and China has placed a multinational corporation, CK Hutchison Holdings, in the middle of strategic rivalry. The case highlights a fundamental contrast between corporate logic and state logic. For a firm, divesting assets may appear to be a rational financial decision to secure liquidity and reduce risk. For states, however, control of strategic infrastructure is often interpreted through the lens of national security. This divergence of perspectives can place multinational corporations in extremely difficult positions when great-power competition intensifies.

Box 3.2 CK Hutchison, the Panama Canal, and the Clash Between Corporate and State Logic

The Panama Canal is one of the world's most strategic trade arteries, linking the Atlantic and Pacific Oceans. For decades, the United States controlled and safeguarded the Canal Zone, recognizing its importance for global trade and U.S. naval mobility. After Panama assumed full control in 1999, the Canal's operations and adjacent port facilities opened to international concessions. Hutchison Whampoa, a conglomerate based in Hong Kong (now part of CK Hutchison Holdings), won contracts in the late 1990s to operate major ports at both ends of the Panama Canal – the Port of Balboa on the Pacific side and Cristóbal on the Atlantic side. At the time, this stirred controversy in the United States, with some politicians raising alarms about a Hong Kong company (with perceived ties to China) managing critical infrastructure in Panama. Hutchison's port operations proceeded, but geopolitical undercurrents persisted: as China's global influence grew, American strategic circles grew warier of Chinese presence near the Canal.

Tensions came to a head in the early 2020s. By this point, U.S.–China rivalry had intensified across many domains. In Panama, Hutchison's long-term port concession became a focal point for U.S. officials concerned about potential Chinese leverage over the Canal. In 2023–2024, under pressure from the United States, Panama's government initiated a review of Hutchison's port concessions, citing compliance issues. This coincided with political rhetoric in Washington questioning whether a Chinese-linked entity should be allowed such proximity to a U.S. strategic asset (Valle et al., 2025). In early 2025, a significant development occurred: Hutchison agreed to sell 80% of its stake in the Panama ports to a consortium led by BlackRock (a major American investment firm). This sale was widely seen as geopolitically driven. U.S. President Donald Trump (in his second term) had openly called for 'wresting control' of the Canal back to U.S. interests and even hinted at potential military action (Valle et al., 2025). The BlackRock-brokered deal effectively transferred control of the ports to U.S.-aligned entities, which American policymakers hailed as a strategic win (Valle et al., 2025).

The Chinese government responded sharply to the developments. Official statements from Beijing accused the United States of coercing Panama into unfair treatment of Chinese enterprises, characterizing the forced divestiture as politically motivated economic suppression. China's Ministry of Foreign Affairs warned that such actions undermined international economic cooperation principles and could deter future Chinese investments in the region. Despite this strong rhetoric, China refrained from direct retaliatory measures, highlighting a calculated diplomatic stance aimed at minimizing broader diplomatic fallout in Latin America (Reuters, 2025).

From Hutchison's perspective, this sequence demonstrates how a company can be squeezed by great-power politics. Hutchison is a publicly traded firm, not an arm of the Chinese state per se, yet because it hails from Hong Kong (now under Chinese security law), it was viewed with suspicion. The company faced an increasingly challenging geopolitical environment: Panama's government questioned the legality of Hutchison's concession, potentially under U.S. diplomatic pressure, while the United States explicitly sought the firm's removal from strategic port operations. Meanwhile, the Chinese government expressed significant concerns over the sale of Hutchison's port stakes to BlackRock, initiating regulatory scrutiny and highlighting risks to national interests, further complicating the company's international position. For Hutchison, divesting was a way to mitigate risk – they received a hefty sum ($1.8 billion) and exited a situation that could have led to protracted legal battles or even asset seizure in a worst-case scenario. For Panama, aligning with U.S. wishes likely brought diplomatic favour (Panama had in 2017 switched diplomatic recognition from Taiwan to Beijing, so balancing relations is tricky).

This case highlights a geopolitical chokepoint risk (the Canal) entangled with geopolitical scrutiny (a Chinese-associated firm deemed a security risk). Hutchison did nothing 'wrong' operationally – indeed, it ran the ports successfully for years. Yet geopolitical dynamics rather than commercial performance ultimately shaped the company's strategic options. As tensions escalated among the United States, China, and Panama, Hutchison found itself caught between competing political pressures. What appeared to be a rational commercial decision – to divest and reduce geopolitical exposure – quickly became entangled in broader strategic competition.

The episode illustrates a fundamental divergence between corporate logic and state logic. For companies, assets such as ports are financial and operational investments designed to generate stable cash flows. For states, however, control over strategic infrastructure is interpreted through the lens of national security and geopolitical influence. When these two logics collide, firms operating in critical sectors may find themselves drawn into great-power politics regardless of their intentions.

Companies are increasingly mapping their supply chains to identify chokepoint dependencies. For instance a consumer electronics manufacturer might realize that most of its products transit through the South China Sea and explore diversifying shipping routes or using alternative ports. Some companies invest in holding more inventory as a buffer against shipping delays at chokepoints, while others are exploring new routes (the Arctic Northern Sea Route or overland rail from China to Europe) to reduce reliance on any single chokepoint. However, alternatives can be limited. The strategic nature of these passages means governments also step in – for example the U.S. Navy patrolling to keep sea lanes open is a form of geopolitical risk mitigation that indirectly benefits companies. The private sector, on its own, often can only partially mitigate chokepoint risk (you can't move the location of the Suez Canal, after all); hence, the focus is on contingency planning. One lesson from Suez 2021 was the value of supply chain agility – firms that could quickly reroute shipments or source from a different region coped better. It also illustrated that geopolitical risk is not always about war or sanctions – even the *threat* of a chokepoint disruption or an accidental blockage is a geopolitical vulnerability due to the geographic concentration of trade (Allianz SE, 2021).

3.2.3 Geoeconomic Risks

Geoeconomic risks refer to geopolitical risks that arise from the use of economic statecraft and the dynamics of geoeconomics. In recent years, geopolitics has increasingly manifested itself through economic instruments. As Edward Luttwak famously observed, 'the logic of conflict remains the same, but the grammar of commerce has replaced the grammar of war' (Luttwak, 1990). Similarly, Hillary Clinton's 2011 speech on economic statecraft signalled the growing centrality of economic tools in foreign policy. As she noted, 'economic statecraft has two parts: first, how we harness the forces and use the tools of global economics to strengthen our diplomacy and presence abroad; and second, how we put that diplomacy and presence to work to strengthen our economy at home' (Clinton, 2011). In this context, states increasingly use economic instruments – such as sanctions, export controls, tariffs, and investment restrictions – to advance strategic objectives.

While economic statecraft focuses on the policy instruments used by states, it does not fully capture the broader structural environment within which these instruments operate. This limitation leads to the concept of geoeconomics. Inspired by Pfeiffer's (2024) work on geoeconomics in international relations, we define geoeconomics as economic statecraft operating within a spatially conditioned structure of interdependence. In other words, geoeconomics describes how economic relations are embedded within a geographical and institutional space in which states compete to shape the rules governing economic interaction. Introducing the concept of geoeconomics into business diplomacy is important because it highlights that geopolitical risks do not arise merely from interstate economic competition. Rather, such risks emerge when economic competition unfolds within specific geographic and institutional environments that shape patterns of interdependence. Only by understanding these spatial settings can firms fully grasp how and why geopolitical risks materialize.

A clear illustration can be found in the competition over global connectivity infrastructure. Initiatives such as China's Belt and Road Initiative (BRI), the European Union's Global Gateway, and the U.S.-led Partnership for Global Infrastructure and Investment (PGII) represent competing geoeconomic visions for organizing international connectivity networks. These initiatives are not simply economic development programs; they involve strategic competition over the control of ports, transport corridors, digital infrastructure, and energy routes. For companies participating in infrastructure, logistics, or energy projects, geopolitical risks arise precisely because these investments are embedded within contested geographic spaces.

Importantly, geography in this context should not be understood purely in physical terms. It also refers to an institutional space – the regulatory frameworks, governance regimes, and norms that structure international economic relations. Economic interdependence between states, therefore, takes place not in a vacuum but within specific institutional arrangements. Competing actors often seek to shape this space in ways that reflect their own strategic and ideological preferences. These tensions are particularly visible in relations between major economic actors such as the European Union, China, and the United States. The European Union officially characterizes China simultaneously as a partner, an economic competitor, and a systemic rival (European Commission, 2019). This triadic characterization reflects the growing recognition that economic relations with China occur within an institutional space whose governance principles are contested.

For multinational corporations, these dynamics create a distinct category of geopolitical risk that we define as geoeconomic risk – corporate exposure to political decisions that reshape economic interdependence within contested physical and institutional spaces. Unlike traditional territorial conflicts, geoeconomic competition operates through economic networks such as trade, finance, technology, and investment regimes. Firms therefore face risks not from physical conflict but from regulatory restrictions, investment screening, technology bans, or sudden changes in market access rules. In such situations, companies may find their operations constrained not because of their commercial performance but because they operate within institutional spaces shaped by competing geoeconomic visions.

The experience of Chinese firms operating in Europe illustrates this form of geoeconomic risk. As geopolitical tensions between China and Western countries intensified, Chinese companies increasingly faced regulatory scrutiny and political resistance in European markets. The suspension of the EU–China Comprehensive Agreement on Investment (CAI) following mutual sanctions in 2021, stricter investment screening mechanisms, and restrictions on companies such as Huawei in European 5G networks all demonstrate how economic relations can become politicized within a contested institutional environment.

These developments highlight how multinational corporations can become exposed to geopolitical risks arising from geoeconomic competition. Companies operating across different regulatory and political systems may find themselves navigating conflicting rules, political narratives, and security concerns. In such contexts, understanding the geoeconomic landscape – how states seek to shape economic interdependence for strategic purposes – becomes essential for anticipating and managing geopolitical risks.

Box 3.3 illustrates how Chinese firms operating in Europe have encountered these geoeconomic dynamics in practice.

Box 3.3 Chinese Firms in Europe: Geoeconomic Competition and the Politicization of Market Access

Over the past two decades, Chinese companies have expanded their footprint in Europe through trade, investment, and acquisitions. This ranges from technology firms like Huawei and ZTE selling telecom equipment, to state-owned companies investing in ports (e.g. COSCO in Greece's Piraeus port), to private investors acquiring European brands (like Geely buying Volvo Cars). Initially, European countries mostly welcomed Chinese business as a source of capital and growth. However, as relations between China and the West soured over issues like market access, human rights, and espionage fears, Chinese firms began encountering increasing scrutiny in Europe – both from governments and the public.

One example is the fate of the EU–China CAI. Launched in 2014 and negotiated over several years, the agreement was concluded in principle in late 2020. It was meant to open up investment opportunities and level the playing field for EU and Chinese companies in each other's markets. But in March 2021, the European Union sanctioned several Chinese officials over human rights abuses in Xinjiang (Reuters, 2021b). China retaliated with its own sanctions on European parliamentarians and scholars. This tit-for-tat led the European Parliament to freeze the ratification of CAI entirely. From a company perspective, the collapse of CAI meant that anticipated new openings for business (e.g. easier investment rules in China for European firms and vice versa) were put on hold indefinitely. Chinese companies that had hoped CAI would ease their expansion in Europe saw those prospects dim.

Moreover, the sanctions episode hardened attitudes: Chinese firms found European regulators more likely to block or scrutinize deals. For instance in 2022, Italy vetoed the acquisition of a semiconductor company by a Chinese investor under its 'golden power' rules, citing strategic security – one of several such blocks across Europe in sensitive sectors.

Huawei's difficulties in Europe illustrate another facet. Europe was a key market for Huawei's 5G telecom equipment. But following the lead of the United States (which banned Huawei), many European governments either banned or heavily restricted Huawei in their 5G networks by 2020–2021, largely due to pressure from the United States and concerns about Chinese law obliging companies to cooperate with state intelligence (Gallagher, 2022). Countries like the UK and Sweden went as far as ordering the removal of the existing Huawei gear. This forced telecom operators (Huawei's clients) to rip out and replace equipment at significant cost (sometimes with government compensation). For Huawei, it meant loss of billions in revenue and a tarnished reputation in a region that once accounted for a large share of its overseas business. Beyond telecom, ideological scrutiny in Europe extends to areas like surveillance technology – for example Chinese camera and AI companies (Hikvision, Dahua) have been accused of abetting human rights abuses (surveillance of Uyghurs) and thus face bans for public procurement in some European locales. Consumer sentiment has also turned in some countries; surveys show growing distrust of Made-in-China tech over data privacy.

On the other side, European and Western firms in China have faced their own ideological tests (like the H&M boycott). But focusing on Chinese firms in Europe, one mitigation strategy has been localization: hiring local executives, emphasizing compliance with EU laws, and storing data in Europe to counteract fears of data transfer to China. TikTok, for example, launched 'Project Clover' to localize data storage in Europe amid regulatory pressure. Huawei opened transparency centres where European officials could inspect source code (an effort to prove they had nothing nefarious). Despite these efforts, some barriers are tough to overcome if geopolitical trust is low.

This case study underscores how geopolitical tensions between states can directly curtail market opportunities for companies. Chinese companies in Europe found themselves constrained not because of their balance sheets but because of foreign policy and value clashes (authoritarian vs democratic systems). The European attitude shift was also about *reciprocity* – European businesses felt unwelcome or unfairly treated in China, so European authorities became less generous to Chinese businesses. In essence, Chinese companies became increasingly constrained by the broader dynamics of EU–China relations.

For Chinese firms (and, more broadly, any company from a country whose government is at odds with a host region), the key lessons are the importance of compliance and transparency to counter stereotypes and the need to prepare for sudden regulatory changes. It also highlights the role of international agreements: had CAI gone through, it might have institutionalized channels to resolve such issues, but without it, each investment became politicized. As geopolitical rivalry persists, Chinese businesses may pivot to other regions perceived as more welcoming (e.g. Middle East, Africa), while Europe in turn is diversifying away from Chinese suppliers in critical areas (the buzzword being 'de-risking' rather than full decoupling).

In sum, Chinese firms in Europe illustrate how geoeconomic competition can transform ordinary market interactions into arenas of strategic contestation, where ideology, security perceptions, and institutional governance override purely economic considerations. Companies must navigate not just laws but public perception and political narratives as well. This case is a mirror image of Western firms in China facing nationalism – in both situations, globalization is constrained by geopolitical mistrust.

These case studies, varied as they are, each highlight the importance of business diplomacy and strategic adaptability. Hutchison Whampoa had to diplomatically navigate U.S.–China tensions in Latin America, Chinese firms in Europe had to adapt strategies to a fracturing political climate, and Western firms in Russia had to make swift strategic shifts to uphold principles and manage losses. In all cases, understanding the geopolitical context – the motives of states, the power of public opinion, the trajectory of conflicts – was crucial. Next, we turn to general methodologies companies can use to systematically identify and anticipate such geopolitical risks before they erupt and then to strategies to mitigate and manage them.

3.3 Identifying Geopolitical Risks at the Company Level

How can companies proactively identify geopolitical risks relevant to their business? Given the wide array of potential issues – from local unrest to global power shifts – a systematic approach is needed to scan the horizon and pinpoint what matters to the firm. Identifying geopolitical risk is fundamentally about recognizing the external political developments that could disrupt the company's geographic footprint or strategic interests. Below are key methods and tools for identifying these risks:

1. **Geographic Risk Mapping:** companies should start by mapping their operations, supply chains, and key markets geographically against known geopolitical hotspots. This involves asking: *Where are our factories, suppliers, distribution centres, and critical customers located? What countries and trade routes do we rely on?* Once mapped, overlay this with information on geopolitical conditions: disputed territories, sanctioned regions, military conflict zones, areas of high political instability. Tools like Geographic Information Systems (GIS) can be used to create visual 'risk maps', highlighting, for example, that a supplier is in a country with rising civil unrest, or a shipping route goes through a volatile strait. For instance a company might map that its electronics are shipped from East Asia to Europe via the South China Sea and Strait of Malacca – immediately flagging that a flare-up in that region could be a risk. Such mapping makes the abstract concept of geopolitical risk concrete and location-specific. Companies like DHL and Maersk have developed global risk maps that rate countries on factors like political stability and conflict; these can guide routing and investment decisions
2. **Stakeholder and Actor Analysis:** identifying geopolitical risks also means identifying *who* might create a risk. Which state or non-state actors have the power to affect your business? For each key country you operate in, consider the government's stance towards foreign businesses, any history of expropriation or sudden regulatory changes, and the relations that country has with your home country. For example a U.S. company doing significant business in Turkey should note that U.S.-Turkey relations have

been strained at times – could that lead to sanctions or popular backlash? Similarly, identify alliances or blocs (the EU, ASEAN, etc.) that might introduce coordinated policies. This actor analysis extends to individuals: are there leaders (presidents, ministers) known for unpredictability or nationalism that could heighten risk? By mapping stakeholders, companies basically emulate intelligence agencies – understanding the interests and possible actions of foreign powers and how those intersect with the company's interests. Some firms establish internal geopolitical monitoring teams or subscribe to political risk intelligence services which provide regular updates on key actors and geopolitical 'risk signals'

3. **Monitoring and Early Warning Systems:** to identify risks in a timely manner, continuous monitoring of geopolitical developments is crucial. This goes beyond reading headlines. Companies are increasingly using specialized geopolitical risk feeds and analytics. For instance geopolitical risk dashboards have emerged as a tool, where companies tier their key markets by risk level and receive monthly updates on each (McKinsey & Company, 2023). A dashboard might show, for example, that 'Market A' moved from medium to high risk this month due to a new law or election outcome, along with notes on what that development is. The board or executives can then question how that affects strategy. Techniques like horizon scanning and media monitoring (using AI to scan news in multiple languages for keywords like 'nationalization' or 'sanctions' related to your locations) can yield early warnings. Some advanced firms leverage Natural Language Processing (NLP) to gauge sentiment in local news or social media about foreign companies, which could foretell brewing nationalist campaigns or regulatory crackdowns (Leslie, 2025). As noted earlier, researchers have even quantified firm-level geopolitical risk by parsing earnings calls for geopolitical mentions (Shen, 2025); similarly, parsing government statements for mentions of industries or countries can indicate if, say, 'tech sovereignty' is becoming a buzzword (implying future local rules). Establishing a dedicated geopolitical intelligence unit or partnering with consultancies and universities is an increasingly common practice to systematically track these indicators
4. **Engagement and Diplomatic Channels:** sometimes, direct dialogue can help identify risks which are not yet public. Companies which maintain close relations with government officials (both at home and in key markets) may receive quiet advisories. For example an ambassador might hint to a multinational CEO that political changes are afoot that could affect foreign investors. Likewise, participating in industry councils or chambers of commerce in-country often gives companies a heads-up on potential policy shifts (as governments may float trial balloons in those forums). This is part of what we term *business diplomacy*: treating political listening and networking as a core part of risk identification. By cultivating a network of contacts – former diplomats on your board, local partners plugged into political circles – a firm can better read the tea leaves of geopolitics. Such

engagement must be done ethically and transparently, but it can be invaluable. For instance companies that were closely following U.S. and EU policy debates in late 2021 likely anticipated tough sanctions on Russia if it invaded Ukraine, while those aloof from policy circles might have been caught off guard by the speed and unity of the sanctions response

5. **Focus on the 'Geo' in Geopolitics:** as emphasized earlier, restoring the geographic focus is vital in risk identification. This means paying attention not just to countries but also to specific *locations* and *routes*. Identify territorial flashpoints relevant to you: are you sourcing minerals from a region near a border dispute (e.g. cobalt from DRC, which borders unstable regions)? Do you have a critical supplier in Taiwan (which is at the centre of U.S.–China tensions)? These geographic nuances can be overlooked if one only does country-level analysis. A country might be stable overall, but if a key highway or port is in a restive province, that's the risk. So drilling down to sub-national geography and transnational corridors is part of the identification process. Using GIS mapping and satellite imagery (often via reports from think tanks or satellite analytics firms) can reveal trends like military build-ups near trade routes or infrastructure projects that could change risk profiles. In one example, shipping companies now monitor satellite data for signs of naval activity or conflict (e.g. in the Red Sea or Persian Gulf) to advise captains on threat levels (Kamali et al., 2024)

To structure these efforts, companies can adopt a step-by-step framework: identify key assets and their locations; identify relevant geopolitical actors and issues in those locations; monitor those issues with predetermined indicators (e.g. election timelines, troop movements, treaty negotiations, social unrest levels); and regularly update assessments. By following such a structured identification process, companies become more risk aware. They create a knowledge base that informs all further steps in risk management. It's analogous to a radar system scanning the environment for storms – you need that radar before you can decide whether to change course or reinforce defences. Identification does not eliminate geopolitical threats, but it does eliminate some of the *surprise* factors, enabling a faster and more calibrated response when something does happen.

3.4 Conclusion: Towards a Company-Centred Approach to Geopolitical Risks

Developing a company-centred approach to geopolitical risk is by no means easy. Traditionally, geopolitical risks have belonged to the realm of diplomats and military strategists. Only as the global environment shifts back towards a more turbulent and uncertain international order are companies forced to confront a world increasingly shaped by geopolitical tensions and disruptions. This new reality requires firms to fundamentally rethink their operating logic and strategic mindset, as geopolitical risks can ultimately pose existential challenges to corporate survival.

In practice, significant intellectual and professional silos exist between business schools and the field of international relations. Similarly, diplomatic and military communities often operate separately from the business world. Yet managing geopolitical risks effectively requires breaking down these silos and building an interdisciplinary approach. Business executives, diplomats, military strategists, and academic researchers must increasingly collaborate in understanding and responding to geopolitical challenges. Such cooperation requires not only a deeper understanding of geopolitical theories but also the ability to apply these insights to the analysis of international business operations.

It is also important to recognize that geopolitical risk represents a probabilistic threat. A crisis may take years or even decades to materialize. However, once it occurs, the consequences can be immediate and existential. Traditional business risk management, which often treats risk as incremental and manageable, may therefore be insufficient in a highly geopolitical environment. Companies must take geopolitical risks seriously and develop strategies to anticipate and mitigate them before they escalate.

Finally, geopolitical risk management operates at two distinct levels: the state level and the corporate level. These two levels are guided by different strategic priorities. States prioritize national security and long-term geopolitical stability, whereas firms prioritize corporate survival and profitability. This divergence can generate tensions between governments and multinational corporations. Companies must therefore remain attentive to the strategic priorities of states, even when these priorities conflict with short-term commercial interests. In this sense, the relationship between states and companies is inherently dialectical. Firms depend on states for regulatory frameworks, security guarantees, and market access, even as state policies sometimes constrain corporate activity. Ultimately, this relationship underscores the central argument of this book: doing business today increasingly requires diplomatic thinking, and diplomacy itself must remain attentive to the realities of global commerce.

References

Allianz SE. (2021, March 26). *The Suez canal ship is not the only thing clogging global trade*. Allianz Economic Research. https://www.allianz.com/en/economic_research/insights/publications/specials_fmo/2021_03_26_SupplyChainDisruption.html

Caldara, D., & Iacoviello, M. (2022). Measuring geopolitical risk. *American Economic Review, 112*(4), 1194–1225.

Clinton, H. R. (2011, October 14). *Remarks to the economic club of New York*. U.S. Department of State. https://web.archive.org/web/20111105205610/http://www.state.gov/secretary/rm/2011/10/175552.htm

Emmott, R. (2021, November 24). *EU extends human rights sanctions, including on Chinese officials*. Reuters. https://www.reuters.com/world/eu-extends-human-rights-sanctions-including-chinese-officials-2021-11-24/

European Commission. (2019). *EU–China: A strategic outlook*. Brussels: European Commission.

Flint, C. (2024). *Near and far waters: The geopolitics of seapower*. Stanford University Press.

Gallagher, J. C. (2022, January 5). *U.S. Restrictions on Huawei Technologies: National security, foreign policy, and economic interests* (Report No. R47012). Congressional Research Service. https://crsreports.congress.gov/product/details?prodcode=R47012

Kamali, P., Koepke, R., Sozzi, A., & Verschuur, J. (2024, March 7). *Red Sea attacks disrupt global trade*. International Monetary Fund. https://www.imf.org/en/Blogs/Articles/2024/03/07/Red-Sea-Attacks-Disrupt-Global-Trade

Kobziev, A., & Bradshaw, M. J. (2016). The impact of geopolitical tensions on energy markets: The case of Crimea's annexation. In M. J. Bradshaw & T. Van de Graaf (Eds.), *Energy security and global politics: The militarization of resource management* (pp. 123–145). Routledge.

Liao, S. (2021, March 31). *Huawei's 2020 revenue growth slows dramatically as U.S. sanctions hit*. CNBC. https://www.cnbc.com/2021/03/31/huawei-2020-revenue-growth-slows-dramatically-as-us-sanctions-hit.html

Luttwak, E. N. (1990). From geopolitics to geo-economics: Logic of conflict, grammar of commerce. *The National Interest*, (20), 17–23. https://www.jstor.org/stable/42894676

Maçães, B. (2025). *World builders: Technology and the new geopolitics*. Cambridge University Press.

Mackinder, H. J. (1904). The geographical pivot of history. *The Geographical Journal, 23*(4), 421–437.

Mahan, A. T. (1890). *The influence of sea power upon history, 1660–1783*. Little, Brown and Company.

Marrow, A. (2025, February 19). *Will Western companies return to Russia as Trump warms up to Putin?* Reuters. https://www.reuters.com/business/will-western-companies-return-russia-2025-02-19/

McKinsey & Company. (2023, October 3). *A proactive approach to navigating geopolitics is essential to thrive*. https://www.mckinsey.com/capabilities/geopolitics/our-insights/a-proactive-approach-to-navigating-geopolitics-is-essential-to-thrive

New Zealand Ministry of Foreign Affairs and Trade. (2021, April 18). *The importance of the Suez Canal to global trade*. https://www.mfat.govt.nz/en/trade/mfat-market-reports/the-importance-of-the-suez-canal-to-global-trade-18-april-2021

Pfeiffer, C. (2024). *Geoeconomics in international relations: Neorealist and neoliberal conceptualizations*. Routledge.

Reuters. (2021a, July 2). *China launches cybersecurity review of Didi after U.S. IPO*. Reuters. https://www.reuters.com/technology/china-cyberspace-administration-launches-security-investigation-into-didi-2021-07-02/

Reuters. (2021b, November 24). *EU extends human rights sanctions, including Chinese officials*. https://www.reuters.com/world/eu-extends-human-rights-sanctions-including-chinese-officials-2021-11-24

Reuters. (2025, February). *China condemns forced sale of Panama port operations as 'economic coercion'* [News article].

Rice, C., & Zegart, A. (2018). *Political risk: How businesses and organizations can anticipate global insecurity*. Twelve.

Shen, L. S. (2025, February 13). *How firms' perceptions of geopolitical risk affect investment* (Current Policy Perspectives No. 25–3). Federal Reserve Bank of Boston. https://www.bostonfed.org/publications/current-policy-perspectives/2025/how-firms-perceptions-of-geopolitical-risk-affect-investment.aspx

Sonnenfeld, J., Tian, S., Sokolowski, F., Wyrebkowski, M., & Kasprowicz, M. (2022). *Business retreats and sanctions are crippling the Russian economy*. SSRN. https://ssrn.com/abstract=4167193

Spykman, N. J. (1942). *America's strategy in world politics: The United States and the balance of power*. New York, NY: Harcourt, Brace and Company.

Valle, S., McGee, S., & Martina, M. (2025, March 5). *BlackRock to buy Hong Kong firm's Panama Canal port stake amid Trump pressure*. Reuters. https://www.reuters.com/markets/deals/ck-hutchison-sell-80-stake-hutchison-ports-group-1777-billion-deal-2025-03-04/

Vo, L. (2014, May 16). *There are anti-Chinese riots in Vietnam. This should really worry Beijing*. Vox. https://www.vox.com/2014/5/16/5720988/vietnam-riots-china-strategy

4 Networks of Support and Influence

Long before the language of networks entered management theory or the mathematics of network science, diplomats had already made networks their core operating tool. The earliest practitioners of diplomacy – whether Venetian envoys in the Ottoman court, French ambassadors at the court of Louis XIV, or Chinese officials managing tributary relations – relied heavily on informal webs of relationships. Their success was rarely dictated by formal negotiation alone. Much of their real work happened informally: in salons, private homes, and quiet backroom discussions where valuable information was exchanged and subtle influence applied. In Renaissance Italy, where the modern diplomatic system first took a recognizable form, city-states like Venice developed sophisticated diplomatic services whose representatives lived for years or decades abroad, cultivating networks of informants, financiers, merchants, and local elites. These relationships extended far beyond official audiences with princes or popes. In the complex and shifting alliances of 16th-century Europe, personal relationships often dictated the speed and substance of information flows more than formal channels. By the 19th century, great European diplomats like Metternich in Austria and Talleyrand in France converted the management of personal networks into high statecraft. Their ability to maintain communication with multiple centres of power; navigate the subtleties of personal relationships among monarchs, aristocrats, and financiers; and build coalitions across borders made them indispensable to their sovereigns. Similarly, the Chinese imperial system for centuries employed tribute missions, where personal relationships with court officials determined the success or failure of foreign envoys far more than formal treaties.

Modern diplomacy still revolves around these principles (Berridge, 2015). While official contacts with foreign ministries remain essential, no effective diplomat limits themselves to government interlocutors. Indeed, the diplomat who confines herself to the host nation's ministries will quickly find herself blind to the full complexity of local power structures. Successful diplomats cultivate journalists, think tank researchers, business leaders, labour union officials, cultural figures, academics, and increasingly, digital influencers. The more diverse their network, the more comprehensive their intelligence and the more resilient their influence (Sharp, 2009).

DOI: 10.4324/9781032625089-5

Perhaps no 20th-century diplomat better embodied the art of building wide-ranging networks than Ivan Maisky, the Soviet Ambassador to London during the tense years leading up to and through the Second World War (Maisky, 2015). Maisky understood that British foreign policy was not shaped solely within the halls of Whitehall. Instead, power and influence were distributed across political parties, newspapers, academia, the labour movement, and the intellectual elite. With great skill, Maisky embedded himself in this broader British ecosystem. He befriended journalists at leading newspapers, dined regularly with members of Parliament from multiple parties, attended cultural events, and engaged with academics and artists who shaped public debate. Through these relationships, Maisky developed not only a sophisticated understanding of Britain's domestic and foreign policy debates but also multiple channels through which he could quietly influence opinion in favour of Soviet interests.

Maisky's diaries (2015) reveal how his network allowed him to gather insights unavailable through formal diplomatic channels. Conversations with Labour Party leaders offered him an early window into evolving British attitudes towards Nazi Germany, long before these shifts were reflected in government policy. Meanwhile, his access to the British press helped him subtly influence public narratives in ways favourable to Moscow. His skilful navigation of British political and intellectual society positioned him as one of Stalin's most effective envoys during the most dangerous years of the 20th century. The Maisky example demonstrates a key truth: in diplomacy, the breadth and depth of one's network can often matter more than one's official status. The diplomat who knows only government officials lacks visibility in emerging social, cultural, and political shifts that may reshape national policy. Similarly, the business leader who limits herself to regulators and commercial partners may find herself dangerously exposed when broader currents turn against her industry.

Diplomatic networks serve two primary purposes: the gathering of information and the exertion of influence. These two functions are deeply intertwined. The diplomat who gathers accurate, nuanced information becomes more effective in advocating her country's interests. Conversely, the ability to exert influence often depends on possessing information that others value or acting as a trusted intermediary who can facilitate mutually beneficial outcomes. Information gathering requires more than monitoring official pronouncements. It demands ongoing conversations with diverse sources, each holding a partial piece of the puzzle. The journalist may provide an early warning of an impending scandal, the academic may offer context on long-term policy trends, and the business leader may reveal which factions within government wield real power. Over time, these fragments accumulate into a sophisticated understanding, unavailable from official briefings alone. Influence, meanwhile, grows from trust built over time. The diplomat who proves a reliable source of insight or assistance finds doors opening more easily. Influence grows incrementally as counterparts come to see the diplomat as a reliable, helpful presence rather than a transient visitor. Ironically, diplomats have a duplicitous reputation ('an honourable man sent abroad to lie for his country'). But as Harold Nicolson (1969) points out, while a diplomat may not be able to tell the whole truth, she should never lie. Once a diplomat is caught lying, she loses her credibility as a source of information and her ability to build networks of influence. The same is true of 'business diplomats'.

Networks and face-to-face contacts serve another vital purpose in modern diplomacy: the identification of intentions. While governments are heavily dependent these days on technological sources of intelligence, whether listening in on communications or breaking into information systems, these often do not provide the key information about the motives or intentions of other actors. Understanding motives and intentions is as important in business as it is in geopolitics. Understanding the intentions of government or commercial actors is essential in developing effective business and risk management strategies. Is a particular piece of legislation designed to damage a business model or is the damage simply the collateral effect of legislation designed to achieve a different end (in which case there may be scope for modifying the legislation to reduce its impact on the said business model)? Recent neurobiological studies have revealed that humans are surprisingly good at accurately identifying intentions, rather better than most of us believe. The key to accurate identification of intentions is regular face-to-face contact. Governments wanting to identify the intentions of other governments need employees who have regular face-to-face contact at senior level with those governments, otherwise known as diplomats. Ironically, the development of digital technologies and the threats of cybersecurity (which we will explore in a later chapter) make this human identification of intentions even more important. The challenges of attribution and the ambiguity of coding (which reveals its intentions only after activation) make the understanding of what foreign governments are seeking to achieve central to successful national security.

While diplomats have instinctively understood the power of networks for centuries, scholars only began analysing them systematically in the late 20th century. For business leaders seeking to apply diplomatic networking principles, it is useful to explore some of these insights. One of the most important came from sociologist Mark Granovetter, who in 1973 published his seminal essay *The Strength of Weak Ties*. Granovetter (1973) challenged the assumption that strong, close relationships were always the most valuable. Paradoxically, weak ties – casual acquaintances, occasional contacts, and distant professional relationships – often provide access to new information and unexpected opportunities. Close contacts often inhabit similar social worlds and see similar information. Weak ties connect us to different sectors, industries, and political spheres. They act as bridges to new domains.

For both diplomats and business executives, this insight explains why networks must be consciously designed for diversity. The CEO who knows only other CEOs risks being blindsided by regulatory shifts or political crises. The ambassador who speaks only to host government officials may miss the early rumblings of popular discontent that will eventually overturn policy. Sir Anthony Parsons recalled how the limits of his contact network in Iran in the later 1970s, fundamentally to the political and commercial elites within the Sha's regime and aimed at promoting the UK´s commercial interests, led him to underestimate the strength of opposition to the Sha in the streets and thus the scale of the threat of regime collapse. The cost to the UK's political and commercial interests was significant and continue nearly 50 years later.

Ronald Burt (1992), another leading scholar of network theory, expanded this argument through his concept of 'structural holes'. Those who sit between disconnected groups – who bridge these structural holes – wield disproportionate influence as brokers. The diplomat who can speak both to conservative generals and progressive opposition activists serves as a conduit few others can replace. One of the authors of this book serves in an embassy in Spain. His colleagues joked that they knew whether he was meeting contacts from the right or the left of Spanish politics according to whether he arrived in the office wearing a suit or jeans. The corporate executive who builds relationships across industries, regulators, media, and academia occupies similar broker positions.

Robust networks are also resilient networks. The more diverse and redundant a network, the better able it is to withstand shocks. If a government collapses, an embassy with deep relationships in media, civil society, and academia remains functional. If a regulator retires, companies with ties to think tanks, journalists, parliamentarians, and multiple agencies maintain institutional access. Digital technologies have amplified these dynamics. Social media, professional networking platforms, and digital public diplomacy tools allow both diplomats and corporations to monitor and influence networks at unprecedented scale. But this proliferation of channels also makes network management more complex: influence now operates both through formal meetings and through fast-moving public narratives. Ultimately, for both diplomats and companies, networks are not static lists of contacts. They are living systems that must be continually cultivated, expanded, and activated as conditions evolve.

For decades, corporate networks primarily served commercial purposes. Companies cultivated relationships with customers, suppliers, regulators, industry associations, and financial partners, focusing on sales growth, regulatory compliance, and operational efficiency. In stable markets with predictable political and legal frameworks, these networks were sufficient. Corporate leaders could confidently leave matters of foreign policy, political risk, and security to governments while they concentrated on business operations. But the business environment has changed dramatically. Globalization, digitalization, and growing geopolitical tensions have exposed companies to complex risks that are no longer purely commercial. Political instability, national security concerns, trade disputes, regulatory shifts, and reputational crises now regularly threaten companies even in historically stable jurisdictions. The commercial network alone no longer offers adequate protection. In this new environment, companies increasingly require networks that resemble those long employed by diplomats. They need contacts not only within ministries of trade and finance but also across parliaments, media organizations, think tanks, advocacy groups, academia, and cultural institutions. Business leaders, like diplomats, must build personal credibility across diverse communities whose decisions, opinions, and influence shape the external environment in which companies operate.

The limits of relying solely on home governments have also become clear. Many national governments lack the reach or influence to protect their companies abroad. In some cases, governments may be conflicted, hesitant to intervene, or even themselves a source of political risk for companies seeking to operate internationally. Moreover, in an era where global business interests may diverge from national security interests, companies increasingly must advocate for themselves and manage their own risk exposure directly. Global companies are thus forced to develop autonomous political capabilities: to gather information, to cultivate influence, to forecast political risks, and to build broad coalitions that can defend their interests across multiple jurisdictions. This transformation marks the emergence of corporate diplomacy as a professional discipline in its own right.

One of the most valuable aspects of a strong network is its ability to function as an early-warning system and a defence mechanism during crises. Reputational risks often arise suddenly and spread rapidly. Allegations of unethical behaviour, environmental damage, data breaches, labour disputes, or political missteps can quickly trigger regulatory investigations, public protests, media attacks, and financial penalties.

Once a crisis has erupted, companies that lack pre-existing relationships with regulators, journalists, advocacy groups, or political actors often find themselves scrambling to build influence in real time. But reputations cannot be defended through ad hoc outreach to strangers. Trusted relationships must be cultivated long before they are urgently needed.

Experienced diplomats have long understood this principle. It is far easier to engage journalists, opposition politicians, or civil society leaders constructively if relationships exist before a crisis. In diplomacy, quiet influence is often exercised behind the scenes through trusted interlocutors whose goodwill has been earned over time.

The same is true for business. When an NGO threatens to launch a consumer boycott, companies with a history of cooperation on sustainability or labour practices may be able to negotiate privately, avoiding damaging public confrontations. When journalists are preparing a critical exposé, those with whom a company has built long-term, open relationships are more likely to provide a fair hearing. When regulators consider imposing fines, prior transparency and open dialogue may earn flexibility and compromise.

Consular work is often the forgotten aspect of diplomacy. Looking after distressed nationals abroad or replacing lost travel documents is not as glamorous as negotiating treaties, preparing political reports, or even promoting companies and their products. But every ambassador knows that it is essential to an embassy's reputation. Nothing will get an ambassador into trouble faster than the failure to protect one of his nationals abroad or not provide the level of service expected (even though consular protection amounts only to ensuring that your citizens are treated no worse than locals: not encouraging in much of the world). Effective consular work is as dependent on building local networks as political or commercial work. But in the case of consular work, these networks are likely to focus on local law enforcement, hospitals, emergency responders, airlines, private security contractors, and logistics providers. Such networks allow consular officers to gather the information crucial to travel and other advice to their nationals (e.g. about local legislation and rules), influence decisions about their nationals (e.g. persuading local law enforcement to treat minor misdemeanours leniently), and ensure support and help from local authorities where needed. Such networks are particularly important in allowing embassies to protect citizens during natural disasters, political unrest, terrorist attacks, or pandemics.

Companies with significant overseas operations must now replicate these capabilities (Henisz, 2017). When instability arises, rapid evacuation of personnel, protection of facilities, and continuity of operations depend on trusted relationships which allow quick access to scarce resources. Airlines, medical providers, security firms, crisis communications experts, and government officials must all be part of a company's extended network long before they are called upon in an emergency. It is no good waiting for the emergency to arrive before seeking help, when those who may be able to offer help may be overwhelmed by events. Identifying the kinds of emergency or crisis that your company might face obviously impacts on the networks you might develop. But a word of caution: crisis prediction is not an exact science. Often, contingency plans are based too tightly on the previous crisis and unravel fast when a new and unforeseen emergency arises. It is because of these uncertainties that the most effective diplomats develop broad contact networks extending beyond the usual suspects, whether the network is developed for political or consular reasons. The COVID-19 pandemic offered a dramatic illustration of these dynamics. As borders closed and supply chains fractured, companies that had invested in strong local networks – with health officials, regulators, transport companies, and local governments – were able to navigate restrictions, secure exemptions, and maintain partial operations far more effectively than those who lacked such relationships. Natural disasters, political protests, coups, sanctions, or targeted violence may strike in any country. Corporate consular-style networks, modelled after embassy practices, offer one of the best defences companies can build against operational disruption (WHO, 2021).

Both diplomatic services and companies face a similar dilemma: the risk of losing network capital when key personnel leave. In embassies, when ambassadors or senior diplomats rotate every few years, their relationships and nuanced personal knowledge often disappear with them. The dilemma is caught in the old joke in foreign ministries – 'the only person worse than my predecessor is my successor' – diplomats can be tempted not to pass on hard won contact networks to their successors. This is often reflected in the frustration of inheriting thin contact books after years of relationship-building have been lost. The private sector faces the same challenge. Executives, country managers, lobbyists, and compliance officers who have built strong political and social networks may retire, change roles, or leave the company, creating gaps that successors struggle to fill. In some cases, these relationships are never fully replaced. To mitigate this risk, leading organizations are increasingly investing in institutionalizing their network knowledge. Some diplomatic services have begun adapting customer relationship management (CRM) software to track personal contacts, record conversations, map indirect connections, and document issue histories. Companies can adopt similar systems, creating global contact management databases that preserve institutional knowledge across teams, regions, and generations of leadership. Properly designed, these systems not only maintain contact lists but also capture the richness of conversations: what was discussed, who introduced whom, what sensitivities were identified, and what leverage exists. Institutionalized networks make organizations more resilient, ensure smoother leadership transitions, and allow companies to avoid having to rebuild influence from scratch with each personnel change.

One way of ensuring greater continuity of contact networks is to make better use of local employees. In both diplomacy and business, locally hired staff often possess the most valuable networks within a country. They are embedded in local society, enjoy trusted personal relationships, and understand cultural nuances and informal power structures in ways expatriates rarely can match. And yet these resources are often not used effectively, either because local staff are seen as in some way inferior to the career expats or because they are not fully trusted. Yet, in embassies, locally employed political or commercial officers may know opposition leaders, union activists, tribal elders, journalists, judges, or business figures who provide vital insights unavailable to foreign diplomats. Their personal reputations often transcend government changes, allowing them to maintain access regardless of political shifts. In multinational companies, local staff may have equally privileged access. The sales manager who plays golf with a cabinet minister, the legal officer married into a politically connected family, the HR executive active in local business associations – these individuals often serve as bridges to otherwise inaccessible power centres. Such relationships can open doors in regulatory agencies, smooth out bureaucratic obstacles, or warn headquarters of brewing controversies.

This is not to say that drawing on the contact networks of local employees is not without problems. It can open up an embassy or company to direct or indirect corruption as the local employee seeks to leverage his position in the embassy or company to seek privileges for friends or family members. Many an embassy has had to resist the efforts of local staff to secure visas for family members. Local employees do not enjoy the protection of diplomatic immunity and so can be open to pressure from local governments or even be subjected to punishment if they are thought to be getting too close to their employers. Ex-pat business executives do not enjoy formal diplomatic immunity, but their position often grants them a kind of informal immunity which their local employees do not enjoy. They should be aware of their potential vulnerability. But although these dangers exist, companies that fail to leverage the political capital of local employees leave substantial value on the table. Wise corporate leaders empower their local teams to contribute to political risk management, influence-building, and relationship cultivation as full participants in the organization's network strategy.

Diplomatic networks reach their highest form when they extend into formal coalitions and alliances. Diplomats constantly work to build multilateral groupings that serve their nations' interests, whether through regional organizations, informal partnerships, or issue-specific alliances. Companies face similar imperatives. On many issues – trade policy, technology standards, data privacy, sustainability, intellectual property, taxation – companies cannot achieve influence alone. They must build coalitions of like-minded companies, industry associations, NGOs, academics, and sometimes governments to advance common goals. Coalitions expand influence by pooling expertise, spreading financial risk, broadening legitimacy, and presenting unified positions to regulators and policymakers. They also allow companies to share information, refine common messaging, and counterbalance adversarial coalitions formed by competitors, activists, or governments. As Churchill said, the only thing worse than fighting with allies is fighting without them.

Traditionally, there have been two approaches to building coalitions: building them around shared values or around shared interests or preferred outcomes. The EU has sought to combine both approaches in building coalitions to promote shared interests with countries that share European values. But this has become increasingly difficult as geopolitical reality has reasserted itself. The tensions between values and interests become too great. Thus, the European Commission has been forced to negotiate with (and praise) the government of Azerbaijan to secure its energy supplies even though that same government had committed widespread ethnic cleansing shortly before in Nagorno-Karabakh. Generally, building coalitions around shared interests or preferred outcomes is a more successful approach than building them around values and more likely to achieve results. Focusing on values can exclude countries from the coalition from the outset that would have been useful (or even crucial) in securing the objectives of the coalition. Focusing instead on shared preferred outcomes, on the other hand, allows the construction of wider coalitions, culturally, politically, and geographically. An example of the latter were the coalitions constructed between countries, companies, and NGOs during the negotiations for the Paris Climate Change Accords. The members of these coalitions did not have to share values or ideologies. They were brought together by agreement on the preferred outcomes they wanted to achieve. The limitations of coalitions based around values have been shown by the failure of the West to isolate Russia diplomatically and economically following its 2022 invasion of Ukraine. Had Western diplomats focused on preferred outcomes, they might have been able to construct a broader and more effective coalition that would have had greater influence on Russian behaviour (Charap & Colton, 2017).

Successful coalition-building requires pragmatism (Wellman & Berkowitz, 1988). In diplomacy, coalitions based on shared interests often prove more durable than those built around rigid ideologies or values. The same holds for business. While companies may express commitments to CSR, sustainability, or human rights, effective coalition-building often centres on converging practical interests rather than idealized alignment on values. Coalitions expand influence by pooling expertise, spreading financial risk, broadening legitimacy, and presenting unified positions to regulators and policymakers. They also allow companies to share information, refine common messaging, and counterbalance adversarial coalitions formed by competitors, activists, or governments. But above all, coalitions are ways of building pressure on decision-makers and influencing them to make decisions that advance the interests of the company. Effective coalitions to influence government policies or legislation are likely to consist of members from a variety of sectoral backgrounds including various kinds of civil society (NGOs, trade unions, academia, etc). Identifying the potential members of such a coalition requires collecting intelligence on the preferred outcome of each potential member as well as considerable networking skills. It also requires lateral thinking in identifying the less likely members who may have nothing in common with the company other than the preferred outcome, which they may prefer for very different reasons. Business diplomats need to remember that other companies, which would be their competitors for market share, may be their allies in seeking stable and fair markets. They must also remember that their own government may not be their best friend and that they may be better working with foreign governments. For example European telecommunications companies seeking to overturn net neutrality in internet governance, a change much in their commercial interest, would do better to work with the U.S. government than with their own national governments or the European Commission.

Few industries have long understood the strategic importance of political networks more deeply than the major international oil companies. For decades, firms like Shell, BP, TotalEnergies, Chevron, and ExxonMobil have operated in some of the world's most politically unstable environments, including Nigeria, Angola, Venezuela, Libya, and Iraq.

In such regions, commercial success depends not only on technical expertise or financial strength but also on the ability to navigate volatile political landscapes. Governments may collapse or change overnight. Nationalization risks loom constantly. Local insurgencies, labour strikes, corruption scandals, or geopolitical sanctions can upend investments within weeks.

Oil executives operating in these environments have long understood that effective networks extend far beyond national governments. In Nigeria, for example, companies operating in the oil-rich Niger Delta have had to cultivate relationships with:

- Federal officials in Abuja responsible for licencing and taxation
- Regional governors and local traditional leaders who control community relations
- Militant groups who periodically attack pipelines and extort payments
- NGOs focused on environmental damage and labour rights
- International human rights organizations monitoring corporate behaviour
- Journalists shaping both domestic and international media narratives

When companies fail to build robust networks, the consequences can be severe. In the 1990s, Shell faced global criticism over environmental degradation and its perceived complicity in Nigeria's brutal repression of activists, including the execution of Ken Saro-Wiwa. The company's weak relationships with civil society actors and its slow recognition of emerging global norms on CSR left it poorly positioned to defend its reputation.

Oil companies operating in Venezuela under both Hugo Chávez and Nicolás Maduro faced similarly complex challenges. Nationalization waves, shifting foreign investment laws, currency crises, and U.S. sanctions forced companies to maintain networks not only with sitting governments but also with opposition parties, international legal advisers, and foreign diplomats who could help negotiate future settlements as political conditions evolved.

The oil industry's long history of navigating fragile states offers important lessons for companies in other sectors now confronting political risk in emerging markets. Networks must extend vertically – from heads of state to local power brokers – and horizontally – across governments, civil society, international institutions, and global media (Frynas, 2000). Only through such diverse relationships can companies remain informed, resilient, and capable of weathering political storms (Pegg, 2012).

In contrast to the oil industry's experience in fragile states, many of today's technology giants – companies such as Google, Meta (Facebook), Amazon, TikTok, and Huawei – face their most intense political and regulatory challenges in highly developed, stable jurisdictions. But stability does not mean predictability. Increasingly, tech companies are finding themselves at the centre of complex debates over privacy, national security, market dominance, data sovereignty, disinformation, and digital infrastructure.

The European Union has emerged as one of the world's most assertive regulators of the global technology sector. Through sweeping legislative frameworks such as the General Data Protection Regulation (GDPR), the Digital Markets Act, and the Digital Services Act, the EU has aggressively sought to reshape how digital platforms operate, not only within Europe but globally as well. The extraterritorial reach of these regulations means that companies worldwide must adapt to European norms or risk exclusion from key markets.

To manage these challenges, American technology giants have built vast influence networks across Brussels and national capitals. These networks include not only formal lobbying with the European Commission but also continuous engagement with national data protection authorities, members of the European Parliament, policy researchers at think tanks, trade associations representing the tech sector, and influential NGOs advocating for digital rights (Kwak, 2021).

Beyond the regulatory sphere, these companies also invest in relationships with academia, funding studies and partnerships that shape public debate on emerging issues such as AI ethics, content moderation, and algorithmic transparency. Simultaneously, public relations teams cultivate relationships with journalists, editors, and public intellectuals who frame narratives about the role of technology in society.

In Washington, the regulatory environment for tech companies has become equally complex, though shaped by different dynamics (Farrell & Newman, 2019). Here, the debate encompasses concerns about content moderation, political bias, privacy breaches, and market concentration. Congressional hearings, state attorney general investigations, Federal Trade Commission lawsuits, and competing legislative proposals have forced companies to develop deep networks across both political parties, federal agencies, advocacy groups, civil liberties organizations, and a highly polarized public discourse.

Chinese technology firms, such as Huawei and TikTok, face perhaps the most acute form of geopolitically charged regulation. Sanctions, national security investigations, and bans in Western markets have forced these companies to invest heavily in influence networks that include local business partners, international law firms, technical standards organizations, former diplomats, and research collaborations with universities. While their efforts have met with only mixed success, they reflect the increasingly diplomatic nature of the challenges facing global technology firms (Segal, 2020).

What unites all of these examples is a simple truth: for technology companies operating at the intersection of commerce, national security, and public trust, the ability to build wide-ranging, multi-layered networks of influence is now as central to business success as product innovation or technical excellence.

The global food and agricultural industry often operates at the intersection of economics, politics, and social stability. Companies such as Nestlé, Cargill, Bayer, and Syngenta not only supply essential goods across borders but also frequently operate in environments where agriculture is tied to national identity, rural employment, land rights, and food sovereignty (Scoones & Thompson, 2011).

Consider the experience of seed and agri-inputs companies operating in India. Regulatory decisions concerning genetically modified crops, fertilizer subsidies, and pesticide approvals are often shaped as much by politics and ideology as by science. Public protests, activist campaigns, and state-level legislative action frequently shape the operating environment.

To navigate this complexity, leading firms have built wide-ranging networks, including relationships with:

- Central and state agricultural ministries and regulatory bodies
- Farmers' unions, many of which have strong political affiliations
- Academic institutions conducting agricultural research
- Environmental NGOs engaged in pesticide and land use debates
- Media outlets shaping rural opinion and national narratives

When India proposed banning several widely used pesticides due to environmental and health concerns, companies with established local networks were able to engage directly with scientific advisers, parliamentarians, and farmer organizations to provide data and propose regulatory alternatives. In contrast, companies lacking such networks faced blanket bans and struggled to recover market access.

During the COVID-19 pandemic, pharmaceutical companies found themselves at the epicentre of global diplomacy. Vaccine manufacturers such as Pfizer, Moderna, AstraZeneca, and Sinovac were not merely selling products; they were negotiating with governments, international organizations, and public health institutions under extraordinary scrutiny and urgency.

Supply chain disruptions, emergency approvals, export controls, and intellectual property waivers all became politically charged issues. In this environment, pharmaceutical companies' ability to activate broad and trusted networks proved critical to their operational success and public standing.

Pfizer's global rollout of its mRNA vaccine required diplomatic engagement with dozens of governments simultaneously. The company worked not only with regulatory bodies such as the U.S. FDA and the European Medicines Agency but also with ministries of health in Africa, Asia, and Latin America. It engaged in real-time conversations with the World Health Organization, COVAX, and the WTO.

Companies with robust, long-standing relationships with public health authorities, academic researchers, and global health NGOs were able to navigate regulatory approvals more smoothly, counter misinformation, and defend their pricing and distribution strategies. Those without such networks, or whose reputations were already fragile, found themselves embroiled in political and media controversies that undermined public trust and led to disruptions.

Luxury brands, cultural industries, and the creative economy are increasingly drawn into geopolitics. Companies such as LVMH, Hermès, Gucci, and Cartier operate across global markets where national pride, identity politics, and cultural sensitivities influence consumer behaviour and regulatory outcomes.

When a luxury fashion house offends national sentiment – by misrepresenting maps, misnaming territories, or mocking local culture – backlash can be swift. In China, several major fashion labels have faced consumer boycotts over perceived slights.

To mitigate such risks, many brands now maintain sophisticated cultural diplomacy networks that include:

- Relationships with cultural ministries and heritage institutions
- Sponsorship of art exhibitions, film festivals, and design schools
- Engagement with local fashion editors, influencers, and brand ambassadors
- Participation in diplomatic events and city branding campaigns

Effective network-building strategies must also adapt to regional political cultures and institutional landscapes.

In Europe, influence requires engagement with national governments, EU institutions, and regional actors. Companies must learn how to navigate Brussels' policy machinery while also maintaining ties to national capitals and regional economies.

In Southeast Asia, ASEAN's principle of non-interference and consensus-based decision-making means that influence operates more informally. Long-standing relationships and face-to-face trust often matter more than formal lobbying.

In sub-Saharan Africa, many companies rely on local political fixers, community leaders, and tribal networks. Government structures may be centralized, but influence is often dispersed across informal power systems.

As geopolitical complexity increases, many leading companies have begun to recognize that network-building is not simply a skill but an institutional capability that must be cultivated systematically. The most sophisticated firms are now building internal structures which mirror the operational models of professional diplomatic services.

First, companies are investing in specialized corporate diplomacy or geopolitical affairs teams staffed not only by experienced lobbyists and compliance officers but also increasingly by former diplomats, intelligence analysts, international lawyers, and risk consultants (Ruël & Saner, 2018). These professionals bring the analytical frameworks, discretion, and negotiation skills honed in the world of diplomacy into the corporate environment.

Second, companies are expanding their external relationship management systems, investing in advanced CRM platforms which map political, regulatory, and civil society contacts across jurisdictions (Saner & Sondergaard, 2000). These systems help track interactions, monitor issue developments, and ensure continuity even as staff rotate.

Third, firms are training senior executives in the fundamentals of international political risk and cross-cultural negotiation, recognizing that CEOs, CFOs, and regional directors may find themselves unexpectedly navigating sensitive diplomatic situations. Increasingly, global companies view political intelligence and influence-building not as side functions, but as core competencies for senior leadership.

Fourth, companies are expanding their participation in international think tanks, academic partnerships, standards bodies, and multilateral forums. These platforms allow companies to shape global debates, build coalitions, and anticipate emerging regulatory trends long before formal policy is enacted.

Finally, companies are recognizing the value of external advisors – retired ambassadors, former regulators, trade negotiators, and regional experts – who can serve as trusted guides through unfamiliar political terrain. These advisors often open doors, interpret opaque power structures, and help companies navigate crises with nuance.

Building these capacities takes time, resources, and careful strategy. But companies that invest in their own diplomatic capacity are better positioned not only to defend their interests but also to shape the evolving global business environment itself.

4.1 Conclusion: The Diplomatic Turn in Global Business

We are living in a world where corporate executives increasingly face challenges that once occupied only foreign ministries and intelligence agencies. Supply chain fragility, sanctions regimes, populist politics, great-power rivalries, regulatory fragmentation, and digital disinformation all intersect with core business operations. As states, markets, and societies become more entangled, companies must think and act like diplomats to survive and thrive.

The lessons of diplomacy offer clear guidance. Networks are not simply repositories of contacts; they are dynamic ecosystems of relationships which must be cultivated with foresight, patience, and creativity. The strength of weak ties, the power of bridging structural holes, and the resilience of diverse networks provide businesses with critical advantages in volatile environments.

Whether navigating an environmental scandal, negotiating with regulators, building multilateral coalitions on climate policy, or responding to a geopolitical crisis, the companies that succeed will be those which have invested in long-term relationships across multiple domains of power. They will have built reservoirs of goodwill that can be drawn upon in moments of uncertainty.

Ultimately, power in the modern world often belongs not to those with the loudest voice, but to those who know whom to call – and who have already invested in building trust before the crisis arrives. In that sense, the diplomat and the corporate leader increasingly share not only challenges but also methods. The diplomat's world has become the business leader's world. And the art of network-building has never been more valuable.

References

Berridge, G. R. (2015). *Diplomacy: Theory and practice* (5th ed.). Palgrave Macmillan.

Burt, R. S. (1992). *Structural holes: The social structure of competition*. Harvard University Press.

Charap, S., & Colton, T. J. (2017). *Everyone loses: The Ukraine crisis and the ruinous contest for post-Soviet Eurasia*. International Institute for Strategic Studies.

Farrell, H., & Newman, A. L. (2019). *Of privacy and power: The transatlantic struggle over freedom and security*. Princeton University Press.

Frynas, J. G. (2000). *Oil in Nigeria: Conflict and litigation between oil companies and village communities*. LIT Verlag.

Granovetter, M. S. (1973). The strength of weak ties. *American Journal of Sociology, 78*(6), 1360–1380.

Henisz, W. J. (2017). *Corporate diplomacy: Building reputations and relationships with external stakeholders*. Greenleaf Publishing.

Kwak, J. (2021). Regulating Big Tech: Policy responses in the United States. *Daedalus, 150*(3), 131–148.

Maisky, I. (2015). *The Maisky diaries: Red ambassador to the Court of St James's, 1932–1943* (G. Gorodetsky, Ed.). Yale University Press.

Nicolson, H. (1969). *Diplomacy*. Oxford University Press. (Original work published 1939).

Pegg, S. (2012). Social responsibility and resource extraction: Are Chinese oil companies different? *Resources Policy, 37*(2), 160–167.

Ruël, H. J. M., & Saner, R. (Eds.). (2018). *The diplomatic dimension of business: Multinational corporations and the public sphere*. Emerald Publishing.

Saner, R., Yiu, L., & Sondergaard, M. (2000). Business diplomacy management: A core competency for global companies. *Academy of Management Executive, 14*(1), 80–92.

Scoones, I., & Thompson, J. (2011). The politics of seed in Africa's Green Revolution. *IDS Bulletin, 42*(4), 123.

Segal, A. (2020). *Huawei and the United States: A test case for 5G* (Special Report No. 87). Council on Foreign Relations.

Sharp, P (2009). *Diplomatic theory of international relations*. Cambridge University Press.

Wellman, B., & Berkowitz, S. D. (Eds.). (1988). *Social structures: A network approach*. Cambridge University Press.

World Health Organization. (2021). *COVID-19 Strategic preparedness and response plan (SPRP 2021)*. https://www.who.int/publications/i/item/WHO-WHE-2021.02

5 Cybersecurity and the Role of Diplomacy in the Digital Battleground

As business diplomats know, former FBI Director Robert Mueller got it wrong when he said that there were only two kinds of companies, those that have been hacked and those who will be hacked. (American Rhetoric, 2012). In reality, there are not two kinds of companies but four: those that have been hacked, those that will be hacked, those who don't know they've been hacked, and those who are not telling the truth about it. In 2022 alone, nearly one billion email addresses were exposed to cybercriminals. The average cost of a data breach reached $4.35 million, and there were 236 million ransomware attacks globally. These figures – already out of date by the time they appear in print – are not just statistics (IBM Security, 2022). They are signposts in a new operational environment in which companies must operate with vigilance, strategy, and resilience. The digital world has become not only a domain of threat, contestation, and vulnerability – but also one where diplomacy can offer new tools for defence and influence.

The exponential growth of digital connectivity has transformed how companies interact with clients, suppliers, governments, and the public. But this transformation has come at a cost. The attack surface has widened; the lines between criminal, activist, and state-sponsored cyber actors have blurred; and the regulatory, reputational, and strategic risks associated with cyber incidents have multiplied. IBM's 2022 Data Security Report highlighted that it takes, on average, 277 days for companies to detect and contain a data breach (IBM, 2022). In a world where a few milliseconds can make the difference in high-frequency trading, nearly nine months of vulnerability is an eternity. And yet, many companies – understandably – prefer to conceal breaches if they think they can. The motivations are clear: protecting share value, retaining client confidence, avoiding supplier panic, and reassuring shareholders. But concealment does not equal control. Denial is not defence.

This is where diplomacy enters the equation. Just as the security of a nation cannot be left to its soldiers alone, corporate cybersecurity cannot be delegated entirely to technicians. Governments increasingly realize that the key issues in cyberspace – from security to internet governance to AI – are not technical but political and geopolitical. Technical problems are relatively

DOI: 10.4324/9781032625089-6

straightforward. Political and geopolitical problems are 'sticky', complicated, and often without a solution. They need diplomatic management rather than technical solution. Firewalls and encryption are essential – but insufficient. A cyber-resilient company must think and act diplomatically, understanding its risk environment, building strategic alliances, managing perceptions, and developing networks of support and influence. Security lies at the heart of diplomacy. From the encrypted communiqués of early embassies to today's concerns about the digital integrity of diplomatic missions, diplomats have long been the stewards of sensitive information and strategic relationships. Their methods – discreet engagement, cross-cultural empathy, careful analysis of intent and capability – are as relevant in cyberspace as they are in geopolitics.

Diplomatic analysis differs from traditional intelligence analysis. Where the latter seeks objective assessment, the former is inherently goal oriented. It examines the intentions behind actions, the perceptions of others, and the means to navigate obstacles and adversaries. Diplomacy is, in this sense, the art of purposeful empathy – seeing the world through the eyes of others and adapting strategies accordingly. This approach has an immediate application to the cyber risk environment. Companies, like countries, must understand their unique threat profile: What do we have that others might want? Who might want it – and why? How skilled and resourced might they be? And, crucially, what coalitions, narratives, or deterrents can we build to raise the cost of an attack and reduce its likelihood?

To apply diplomacy to cyberspace, we must first understand the nature of the threat. While headlines tend to focus on data theft and ransomware, the typology of cyberattacks is far broader:

- **Degeneration**: cyberattacks which cause permanent damage to information or operating systems. When targeted against operating systems controlling physical infrastructure, they can cause damage in the physical world (kinetic impact) including human casualties. The Stuxnet attack against the Iranian nuclear fuel processing plant in Natanz would be an example of a degeneration attack (Zetter, 2014).
- **Disruption**: cyberattacks which aim to disrupt information systems without causing permanent damage. Distributed Denial of Service (DdoS) attacks take control of neutral computers and then direct them to seek information from a targeted webpage, overwhelming its ability to respond and thus crashing it. An example would be the 2007 attack on key webpages in Estonia by Russian activists (Ottis, 2008). Ransomware attacks freeze computers and then demand payment for the key to release the data. Increasingly, such attacks also steal sensitive data and threaten to release it to put further pressure on the victim. Disruption attacks can be criminally or politically motivated.
- **Espionage**: cyberespionage is the removal of data from an information system without the permission of the owner. This can include sensitive

personal data, government secrets, intellectual property, or financial information. As, in a digital financial system, money is also essentially data, this can also include straightforward financial theft. These operations may be criminal, corporate, or state-sponsored. An example of the latter would be the attempt by North Korea´s Lazarus Group to steal 100 million dollars from the central bank of Bangladesh (Das & Spicer, 2016).
- **Disinformation**: the use of digital tools, including deep fakes, to mislead, embarrass, or manipulate public perception. While we think of disinformation operations as primarily government inspired, they can also be carried out by activist groups and criminals.

With the exception of degeneration, each of these attack types can serve both criminal and political agendas. The lines are not always clear. The infamous NotPetya ransomware attack, for example, presented itself as criminal but with no functioning mechanism for ransom collection (the link to pay the ransom did not work) (Blank Rome LLP, 2023). Lawyers representing insurance companies have used this to argue that the attacks were politically motivated and therefore acts of war and not covered by the victims' cyberinsurance problems (Business Insurance, 2024). The courts have yet to rule definitively on the implications for insurance liability – leaving companies in legal and financial limbo (Greenberg, 2018). Moreover, companies can become the unintended victims of broader geopolitical campaigns. Just as a warplane may accidentally bomb a foreign-owned factory in wartime, a cyberweapon aimed at a government may damage private firms along the way. This makes the distinction between primary and collateral targets increasingly meaningless. This may again have happened with the NotPetya attack, which seemed to be targeted primarily at Ukrainian companies, but then spread more widely, including damaging Russian companies.

Diplomacy has long accepted that every country has its own interests, threat perceptions, and strategic objectives. A previous chapter has argued that business diplomacy, and especially the analysis of geopolitical risk, must be company-centric. The same is true in cyberspace. No two companies are alike in their digital exposure, their value to potential attackers, or their vulnerability to specific techniques. Cybersecurity must therefore begin with a company-centric analysis focusing on the following questions:

- What digital assets do we hold?
- What is their value – to us and to others?
- Who might seek to access or destroy them?
- What means and resources would they be likely to use?

For example a pharmaceutical firm developing a breakthrough drug has a different cyber risk profile than a hotel chain. The former may be targeted for its intellectual property by competitors or state-backed actors; the latter may face data theft or reputational risk. Consequently, the cost-benefit calculus for attackers – and defenders – will differ accordingly. Getting this calibration right is vital. Overspending on cybersecurity can starve a company of funds for innovation or expansion. Underspending, on the other hand, can be catastrophic. Strategic diplomacy, applied in cyberspace, can help identify both the appropriate threat level and the most cost-effective defensive strategy.

Despite the sophistication of modern cybersecurity tools, most successful attacks do not involve technological brilliance. They exploit human weakness – reused passwords, unpatched systems, or a moment of inattention on a Friday afternoon. The 2015 WannaCry attack, which paralysed hospitals across the UK, succeeded largely because systems had not been updated with a Microsoft security patch that had been available for weeks (Cybersecurity and Infrastructure Security Agency, 2017). Phishing remains the most common attack vector. Increasingly sophisticated spear phishing attacks, using AI to tailor emails designed to convince the victim to open or download malware in an email attachment, are a growing problem. But even advanced threats rely on human failings. Dissatisfied or careless employees, both current and former, represent a major vulnerability. Here again, diplomacy has lessons to offer.

Diplomatic services have long understood that operational security is as much about morale, loyalty, and culture as it is about encryption and locks. In embassies, every staff member – including local hires – is socialized into a shared security culture. Everyone is not only a potential weakness – but also a potential guardian. Companies, by contrast, often treat cybersecurity as the sole responsibility of an IT department or dedicated security team. This siloed approach is dangerous. Cybersecurity is now a horizontal issue. Every employee – from the CEO to the intern – must understand the stakes and the methods of defence. This is particularly urgent for companies with international operations, where cybersecurity cultures may vary widely. A globally integrated workforce demands globally coherent security values. Diplomacy, with its long experience in cross-cultural engagement, provides a model.

Cybersecurity cannot be achieved in isolation. Threat actors are networked. So must be the defenders. The previous chapter argued that companies that may be competitors for market share can also be allies in managing geopolitical risk. The same is true in cyberspace. The traditional instinct of companies has been to compete – sometimes even on security grounds. But in cyberspace, collaboration often trumps competition. Companies operating within the same sector are likely to share the same cybersecurity profile, with similar risks, threats, and hostile actors. Within sectors, companies can and should form coalitions to share threat intelligence, coordinate responses, and advocate for protective regulation. Governments are essential partners in this process – but cannot be relied on entirely. Cybercrime crosses borders with ease, while law enforcement does not. Diplomatic engagement with government actors can help shape regulation, build public–private trust, and ensure that corporate interests are reflected in national and international cybersecurity strategies.

A previous chapter discussed supply chains and the extent to which these can become geopolitical risks for companies. One aspect of this is the level of cybersecurity in the companies constituting the supply chain. The main company may maintain high levels of cybersecurity, with high levels of technical protection and staff awareness/training. But this can be undone if other companies constituting the supply chain do not maintain similar standards. At worst, hackers may use weaknesses in a subsidiary's cybersecurity to access the information systems of the main company. Even if the main company has protected against this, hackers can gain access to sensitive information that had to be propagated through the supply chain or use the hacking of a subsidiary company to damage the reputation and call into question the reliability of the main company. We have spoken before about socialization, whereby diplomats socialize new international actors into the culture and norms of diplomatic international behaviour. Over the last century, this has seen a series of revolutionary actors being socialized into behaving like standard diplomats. This also has an important role in supply chains, where subsidiary companies are socialized into the culture of the parent company, whether in relation to environmental and social governance (ESG) or cybersecurity.

Yet, the diplomatic opportunities extend further. Again, as argued in the previous chapter for managing broader geopolitical risks, companies in cyberspace can and should build networks of information and influence that include:

- Other companies in the same or adjacent sectors
- Private cybersecurity firms
- Universities and think tanks conducting threat analysis
- Non-governmental organizations working on digital rights, privacy, and policy
- International forums and standards bodies

These networks serve multiple functions: early warning, collective lobbying, narrative shaping, and coordinated response. Crucially, they must be maintained proactively – not just activated in crisis. As we saw in a previous chapter, the tools of business diplomacy – empathy, relationship-building, narrative control, and alliance formation – are equally applicable here.

Governments have been slow to engage with cyberspace diplomatically – but that is beginning to change. The Budapest Convention on Cybercrime remains the only binding international treaty in force, and many significant countries have not signed it (Council of Europe, 2001). A new UN Convention is under negotiation, but its contours remain uncertain (United Nations, 2024). These processes matter. The outcome of international cyber negotiations will shape the legal and regulatory environment in which companies operate. Issues such as data sovereignty, cross-border investigation rights, encryption standards, and liability in the event of attacks all have direct implications for business. Companies that wish to influence these outcomes must be present in the conversation. That does not mean formal participation – but it does mean lobbying, coalition-building, and strategic engagement. It means forging heterogenous networks of state and non-state actors around shared preferred outcomes. As methods of international negotiation and diplomacy evolve, it may mean even more direct participation. A later chapter will discuss the extent to which governments increasingly treat technology companies as geopolitical actors in their own right. In short, it means practising cyberdiplomacy – not only in defence of the company's digital integrity but also in pursuit of a more stable, predictable, and resilient cyberspace.

The abstract nature of cybersecurity risk often makes it difficult for company leaders to grasp the full weight of the threat – until it materializes. In diplomacy, theory must be grounded in experience. The same is true in business diplomacy. To understand the practical value of a diplomatic approach to cyber risk, we must examine how real companies have been affected by cybercrime and how they responded – successfully or not. These examples underscore not only the technical nature of the threat but also the strategic, political, and reputational dimensions which demand a diplomatic mindset.

Perhaps no incident more clearly illustrates the blurred lines between political and criminal cyber activity than the NotPetya attack of 2017. Originally targeting Ukrainian systems, the malware masqueraded as ransomware but lacked any functional payment mechanism. Experts quickly concluded that the real objective was not extortion but destruction. What began as a politically motivated disruption of Ukrainian infrastructure spread far beyond its borders, impacting multinational companies with no direct stake in the conflict.

Maersk, the Danish shipping giant and one of the largest container shipping firms in the world, found its global operations crippled in a matter of hours. Its entire IT infrastructure had to be rebuilt, including 4,000 servers, 45,000 PCs, and thousands of applications. The total financial cost exceeded \$300 million, but the reputational damage and logistical chaos – at ports, in transit, and among clients – was incalculable. Merck, the American pharmaceutical firm, was similarly hit, with production and research delayed across multiple sites, costing hundreds of millions. FedEx's European subsidiary TNT Express was brought to a standstill. Mondelez International, Reckitt Benckiser, WPP, and Saint-Gobain also reported heavy losses.

From a diplomatic standpoint, NotPetya offered a sobering lesson: even companies not directly involved in a geopolitical conflict can become casualties of it. The attack was eventually attributed to Russian military hackers by several Western governments, but attribution did little to help the affected firms recover losses. Insurance claims were denied in some cases on the grounds that the attack constituted an act of war – something not covered under standard policies. Here, the lack of clear international norms and legal consensus on cyber attribution left companies exposed. A more active diplomatic engagement – between firms, insurers, and governments – might have facilitated compensation mechanisms, regulatory reforms, or clearer frameworks for accountability.

Just weeks before NotPetya, the WannaCry ransomware worm burst onto the global stage. Exploiting a Windows vulnerability known as EternalBlue – reportedly developed by the U.S. National Security Agency and leaked by a hacker group – the malware rapidly infected more than 300,000 systems across 150 countries. Victims ranged from Spanish telecommunications firm Telefónica to German railways, Chinese universities, and multiple Fortune 500 companies.

But it was in the UK that the human impact became most apparent. Dozens of National Health Service (NHS) hospitals were forced to cancel surgeries and turn away patients. The chaos was not caused by cutting-edge hacking techniques but by basic administrative oversight. Many NHS systems had failed to install a critical Microsoft security patch released weeks earlier. As a result, hospital operations were brought to a halt – revealing how the simplest vulnerabilities can be the most devastating (National Audit Office, 2017).

The diplomatic implication here is twofold. First, security culture matters. If staff and leadership had been better socialized into a culture of digital hygiene – akin to the discipline instilled in diplomatic services – such an attack might have been mitigated or prevented. Second, it highlighted the need for stronger international collaboration in managing digital infrastructure. The vulnerability used in the attack had originated in a Western intelligence agency; its failure to contain the leak contributed to a global crisis. In such a context, corporate diplomats must engage in broader conversations about cyber norms, digital tools proliferation, and state responsibility.

In May 2021, JBS S.A., the world's largest meat processing company, faced an attack that sent shockwaves through global food supply chains. A sophisticated ransomware group known as REvil infiltrated the company's systems in North America and Australia, forcing the shutdown of multiple plants. The attack jeopardized nearly 20% of America's beef and pork production capacity.

JBS eventually paid an $11 million ransom in Bitcoin to regain access to its systems. The incident immediately became a matter of national concern. The U.S. government, already under pressure from the Colonial Pipeline attack just weeks earlier, attributed the attack to actors likely based in Russia. Diplomatic communications were initiated between the U.S. and Russian governments, urging them to crack down on criminal groups operating from their territory (Statt, 2021).

For JBS, the diplomatic lesson was stark: companies that provide critical infrastructure – whether energy, food, or transportation – operate in a geopolitical environment whether they acknowledge it or not. Cyber resilience is not just an IT issue; it is a matter of national interest. Business diplomacy in such cases involves engaging with law enforcement, regulators, foreign ministries, and even intelligence communities. It also means being part of multistakeholder coalitions that can advocate for stronger deterrents, clearer international rules, and faster mechanisms for cross-border incident response.

5.1 Colonial Pipeline: From Password to Panic

Just days before the JBS breach, the United States witnessed one of the most high-profile cyber incidents in its history. The Colonial Pipeline, which supplies nearly half the fuel consumed on the East Coast, was hit by a ransomware attack that disrupted service for several days. Panic buying ensued, with long queues at gas stations across multiple states. Colonial paid the $4.4 million ransom in Bitcoin – some of which was later recovered by the U.S. Department of Justice.

Investigations revealed that the breach originated with a single compromised VPN password. The attackers, known as DarkSide, exploited a gap in security protocols which allowed them to access Colonial's systems and disable key services. The impact was so severe that the White House declared a state of emergency in 17 states.

This case vividly demonstrates how a single point of failure can cascade into national-scale disruption. For business diplomats, it provides a blueprint for how companies must approach cyber risk: by viewing themselves not just as isolated entities, but as nodes in a broader ecosystem. Engagement with regulators, law enforcement, and civil society becomes essential – not only during crises but also as part of a long-term strategy of mutual resilience.

In contrast to the ransom payments made by Colonial and JBS, the Norwegian aluminium producer Norsk Hydro chose a different path. In March 2019, the company was hit by LockerGoga ransomware, which encrypted files and disrupted operations across 170 sites in 40 countries. Rather than pay the ransom, Hydro opted to restore systems from backups and continue operations manually where possible. The recovery process was slow and costly – estimated at over $70 million – but the company gained widespread admiration for its transparency and ethical stance.

Hydro's handling of the crisis became a model of corporate responsibility. The company held regular press briefings, shared details of the attack and its response, and collaborated openly with cybersecurity experts and public agencies. While operations were impacted, the company's brand and shareholder confidence remained largely intact.

The diplomatic insight here is powerful: narrative control is a strategic tool. Transparency, when managed properly, can enhance trust, reinforce corporate values, and inspire stakeholder solidarity. Business diplomats play a vital role in shaping such narratives – internally and externally – and in mobilizing allies during times of crisis.

In June 2024, a ransomware attack brought down CDK Global, the software provider used by thousands of car dealerships across North America. The breach disrupted sales, financing, and customer relationship systems across the automotive industry. CDK reportedly paid a ransom of $25 million in cryptocurrency, but the damage – operational and reputational – was already done. Dealerships lost millions in daily revenue; lawsuits and regulatory investigations soon followed.

CDK's case reveals a key vulnerability in modern business operations: dependency on digital suppliers. Just as companies once had to secure their physical supply chains, they now must secure their digital ecosystems. Business diplomacy here involves engaging with partners to ensure shared cybersecurity standards, coordinated incident response plans, and mutual transparency. It also involves influencing industry-wide norms and certifications for third-party security.

In April 2025, British retailer Marks & Spencer (M&S) became the victim of a cyberattack believed to be orchestrated by Scattered Spider, a group known for targeting Western firms through social engineering and third-party access. The attackers demanded a ransom, threatening to release sensitive customer data. M&S, a long-standing advocate of ESG, was reportedly targeted due to its high-profile and integrated digital platforms (The Guardian, 2025).

The attack forced the company's online sales systems offline for several days, resulting in millions in lost revenue and a sharp drop in share price. It also prompted questions about how companies with strong ESG credentials might be seen as symbolic targets – much like diplomats operating in hostile political environments.

This underscores the need for corporate diplomacy not just at the technical level but also at the strategic and narrative levels. Companies must be prepared to engage in public debate, to defend their values, and to use their networks – of customers, suppliers, and regulators – to push back against politically or ideologically motivated attacks.

The preceding examples made clear how devastating cybercrime can be. Yet, while threats are increasing in frequency and complexity, so too are the resources available to companies willing to approach cybersecurity with diplomatic foresight. Business diplomacy, as this book argues, is more than image management or stakeholder appeasement. It is a method of strategic influence and coordination, deployed to reduce risk, build alliances, shape regulation, and manage reputations in times of uncertainty.

In the realm of cyber threats, business diplomacy offers five concrete functions:

1. *Building trust-based coalitions across sectors and borders*
2. *Engaging governments as strategic partners rather than distant regulators*
3. *Creating internal security cultures rooted in shared responsibility*
4. *Shaping public narratives through transparency and coherence*
5. *Influencing standards and norms at the international level*

In the increasingly contested space of cyberspace, companies have begun to realize that technical defences are not enough. It is not firewalls alone but also relationships, foresight, credibility, and cross-border cooperation that make the difference between vulnerability and resilience. In this section, we turn to specific case studies to show how business diplomacy – carefully cultivated and actively practised – has enabled companies to withstand, deflect, or even help shape the cyber risk environment. These are not hypothetical scenarios, but real-world illustrations of diplomacy as strategy.

Few companies have learnt the importance of diplomacy in cyberspace more viscerally than Maersk. In June 2017, the Danish shipping giant became one of the most prominent victims of the NotPetya cyberattack. The malware, disguised as ransomware but later judged to be a politically motivated operation originating in Russia, crippled Maersk's global operations in a matter of hours. Its entire IT infrastructure had to be rebuilt. Over 45,000 PCs, 4,000 servers, and a multitude of proprietary applications were taken offline. For a logistics company with a global network of ports, containers, and supply chains, this amounted to a digital heart attack.

But Maersk's response went beyond crisis management. Recognizing that the threat landscape was deeply entangled with geopolitical forces, the company began to build strategic relationships with key institutional actors. Maersk quietly cultivated partnerships with Denmark's national cybersecurity agencies and with NATO's Centre of Excellence for Cooperative Cyber Defence. Its executives took part in cyber defence simulations hosted by NATO, particularly those modelling attacks on global supply chains and port infrastructure.

Through this diplomatic engagement, Maersk gained not only an early access to cyber threat intelligence but also a seat at the table in European regulatory discussions. It was able to influence the framing of future cyber resilience mandates for maritime infrastructure. What began as a devastating breach became an opportunity to reposition Maersk as a strategic partner in European cyberdefence – an example of business diplomacy converting crisis into capital.

In 2018, Siemens took a bold step in international cyber governance by founding the Charter of Trust, a multilateral initiative that brought together some of the world's most influential companies, including IBM, Cisco, Allianz, Airbus, and TÜV Süd. The aim was not merely to issue another corporate statement, but to create a framework for operational principles that could be shared, applied, and eventually codified into international standards.

Through a year of structured dialogue, Siemens and its partners developed a set of guiding principles – secure-by-design architecture, mandatory certification for critical components, joint responsibility for cyber risk, and cooperative incident response protocols. The Charter of Trust was not a response to any single cyberattack, but to the broader realization that a fragmented approach to digital security left all companies exposed.

Siemens led this initiative as a diplomatic actor: convening across sectors, brokering shared language among technical and policy communities, and taking the Charter into forums such as the Munich Security Conference and G20 Digital Ministers' meetings. The result was not just the formation of a trusted alliance but also a tangible influence. Several European and Asian regulatory frameworks now reflect the principles first articulated by the Charter of Trust. Siemens, by shaping the rules of the game, positioned itself as both a thought leader and a preferred supplier in an era of rising digital insecurity.

During the 2022 Russian invasion of Ukraine, the role of business diplomacy in cyberspace reached new dimensions. Microsoft, through its Digital Threat Analysis Center (DTAC), played a pivotal role in defending Ukraine's digital infrastructure from relentless cyberattacks. These were not simple data breaches, but strategic attempts to wipe data, disable public services, and destabilize the country's administrative backbone (Microsoft, 2022a).

Microsoft's response was multifaceted and deeply diplomatic. First, it established direct communication with Ukrainian government officials and CERTs (Computer Emergency Response Teams), sharing intelligence on malicious software campaigns, notably the FoxBlade wiper malware, even before it was used. It offered its secure cloud infrastructure to Ukrainian ministries and helped migrate critical data off compromised on-premise servers (Microsoft, 2022b).

Beyond operational support, Microsoft became an advocate for international norms. President Brad Smith publicly called for a Digital Geneva Convention to prohibit cyberattacks on civilian infrastructure. The company's lobbying efforts reached the UN, the EU, and NATO, urging for more robust governance of cyber conflict. This combination of immediate operational assistance, policy engagement, and global advocacy made Microsoft a textbook case of cyber diplomacy in action – showing that corporations, too, can act as diplomatic agents in theatres of geopolitical tension.

Telefónica, the Spanish telecommunications giant, recognized early the need to approach cybersecurity not only through technical safeguards but also through shared norms and industry-wide cooperation. As one of the original signatories of the Cybersecurity Tech Accord – an initiative now supported by over 150 global firms including Microsoft, Cisco, Ericsson, and HP – Telefónica pledged to defend all customers against malicious cyber activity, regardless of geopolitical origin or motive.

This commitment wasn't merely symbolic. Telefónica used its standing in Europe and Latin America to promote the Accord's principles in legislative discussions, especially around Europe's Digital Services Act and Spain's national cybersecurity strategies. It also led workshops and webinars for public-sector CIOs across Latin America, highlighting how private firms could be partners – not just targets or vendors – in national digital resilience.

Through this proactive diplomacy, Telefónica strengthened its reputational capital. It was seen not only as a service provider but also as a responsible steward of cyberspace. This perception helped the company secure long-term contracts with public institutions and avoid overbearing regulation by building trust before crises arose.

Operating in over 100 countries, many of them in volatile regulatory environments, Nokia faced a complex cyber diplomacy challenge: how to promote secure-by-design telecommunications infrastructure in markets where cybersecurity regulation was nascent, uneven, or politically sensitive.

The company addressed this not by withdrawing, but by leaning in. In Kenya, Indonesia, and Brazil, Nokia signed memorandums of understanding with national CERTs to support joint incident response, training, and knowledge exchange. It co-hosted cyber hygiene campaigns and technical hackathons with local universities, helping build a pipeline of cybersecurity professionals.

Simultaneously, Nokia offered its expertise to national regulators, helping them draft telecom-specific cybersecurity frameworks. This not only ensured that its products would meet evolving standards but also positioned Nokia as a trusted policy partner – mitigating the risks of future regulatory backlash or exclusion.

This approach – rooted in respect, collaboration, and shared investment in cyber capacity – demonstrated how a multinational could practise diplomacy at the edge of state authority, shaping environments where laws and institutions were still fluid.

In April 2022, India's CERT-In introduced a sweeping new directive requiring all companies to report cybersecurity incidents within 6 hours – a timeline far shorter than global norms. For multinational firms, this posed logistical and legal challenges, particularly for incidents that spanned jurisdictions or required board-level review.

Rather than confronting the Indian government publicly, companies such as Amazon, Google, and Cisco engaged diplomatically through national industry associations and international business chambers. They initiated private dialogues with Indian authorities, providing technical justifications for extending compliance timelines and clarifying ambiguous reporting requirements.

This quiet diplomacy paid off. CERT-In issued clarifications, softening some of the more onerous provisions, and gave certain industries a phased compliance timeline. By engaging respectfully and constructively, these companies were able to influence regulatory practice without provoking political defensiveness – underscoring the value of patient, behind-the-scenes diplomacy in managing regulatory risk.

Diplomacy is not always external. At Infosys, one of India's largest IT services firms, a successful cybersecurity strategy was built internally. With over 300,000 employees, the company recognized that its biggest vulnerability was not code but people.

In response, Infosys launched the CyberSAFE programme – an internal initiative that gamified cybersecurity training, rewarded responsible behaviour, and designated 'security ambassadors' in every business unit. These ambassadors were trained not only in security protocols but also in communication and leadership, empowering them to act as internal diplomats for security culture.

The result was a measurable drop in successful phishing attacks and a dramatic rise in incident reporting by staff. By embedding cybersecurity into the social fabric of the company, Infosys reduced its risk profile and enhanced its attractiveness to clients who viewed strong internal governance as a key metric in supplier selection.

Mastercard, operating in a high-stakes environment where cyber breaches can ripple through the global financial system, recognized early the importance of coordination. It established a series of regional risk councils – confidential forums bringing together banks, fintech firms, regulators, and cybersecurity experts.

These councils did not meet in response to crises alone. They planned for them as well. They conducted joint exercises simulating ransomware attacks, card system disruptions, and data exfiltration. After real-world breaches, such as the Equifax or Capital One incidents, Mastercard hosted debriefs to ensure that lessons were shared and mitigation strategies improved.

This model of ongoing dialogue, scenario planning, and mutual trust is classic diplomacy – though conducted in the language of finance and data rather than treaties and protocols. Through these councils, Mastercard positioned itself not only as a financial platform but also as a diplomatic nexus – a convenor of interests united by shared vulnerability and shared ambition for resilience.

These examples demonstrate that business diplomacy is more than good public relations. It is an indispensable component of corporate cybersecurity strategy. In each case, the companies that fared best were those that had built:

- *Networks of influence* that included regulators, industry peers, and civil society.
- *Reputational capital* that allowed them to take strong public stances or recover quickly from crisis.
- *Internal cultures* that treated security not as a department but as a shared ethic.
- *Global awareness* of how geopolitics and regulation affect their digital risk environment.

In today's threat landscape, companies cannot buy cybersecurity off the shelf. They must cultivate it through relationships, foresight, and strategic engagement. In this, business diplomacy proves itself not just useful – but essential as well. The digital world has transformed not only how companies do business but also how they must think about risk, resilience, and influence. Cybersecurity is not a purely technical challenge. It is a strategic one – and increasingly a diplomatic one. By applying the tools of diplomacy – empathetic analysis, cultural adaptation, strategic networking, coalition-building, and narrative control – companies can strengthen their cyber defences and shape the environment in which they operate.

References

Blank Rome LLP. (2023, January 13). *Appellate division affirms trial court ruling that "war risk" exclusion does not apply to NotPetya attack*. Blank Rome Insurance Recovery Blog. https://insurerecovery.com/merck-notpetya-appeal/

Business Insurance. (2024, March 22). *Mondelez, Zurich settle cyber war exclusion case*. https://www.businessinsurance.com/article/00010101/NEWS06/912358404

Council of Europe. (2001, November 23). *Convention on cybercrime* (ETS No. 185). https://www.coe.int/en/web/conventions/full-list/-/conventions/treaty/185

Cybersecurity and Infrastructure Security Agency. (2017, May 12). *Indicators associated with WannaCry ransomware*. https://www.cisa.gov/news-events/alerts/2017/05/12/indicators-associated-wannacry-ransomware

Das, K. N., & Spicer, J. (2016, July 21). *How the New York Fed fumbled over the Bangladesh Bank heist* [Special report]. Reuters. https://www.reuters.com/investigates/special-report/cyber-heist-federal/

Greenberg, A. (2018, August 22). *The untold story of NotPetya, the most devastating cyberattack in history*. WIRED. https://www.wired.com/story/notpetya-cyberattack-ukraine-russia-code-crashed-the-world/

The Guardian. (2025, April 23). *Marks & Spencer cyber-attack disrupted online sales for days*. https://www.theguardian.com/business/2025/apr/23/marks-and-spencer-cyber-attack-online-sales

IBM. (2022, July 27). *Cost of a data breach report 2022* [Press release]. https://newsroom.ibm.com/2022-07-27-IBM-Report-Consumers-Pay-the-Price-as-Data-Breach-Costs-Reach-All-Time-High

Microsoft. (2022a, June 22). *Defending Ukraine: Early lessons from the cyber war*. https://www.microsoft.com/security/blog/2022/06/22/defending-ukraine-early-lessons-from-the-cyber-war/

Microsoft. (2022b, April 27). *Special report: Ukraine – An overview of Russia's cyberattack activity in Ukraine*. https://www.microsoft.com/en-us/security/security-insider/threat-landscape/special-report-ukraine/

Mueller, R. (2012, March 1). *RSA cyber security conference address*. American Rhetoric. https://www.americanrhetoric.com/speeches/robertmuellerrsacyberconference2012.htm

National Audit Office. (2017). *Investigation: WannaCry cyber attack and the NHS*. https://www.nao.org.uk/wp-content/uploads/2017/10/Investigation-WannaCry-cyber-attack-and-the-NHS-Summary.pdf

Ottis, R. (2008). Analysis of the 2007 cyber attacks against Estonia from the information warfare perspective. In *Proceedings of the 7th European Conference on Information Warfare* (p. 163). Reading, MA: Academic Publishing Limited.

Statt, N. (2021, June 10). *JBS paid $11 million after cyberattack, according to WSJ*. The Verge. https://www.theverge.com/2021/6/10/22528162/jbs-paid-11-million-ransomware-attack-wsj

United Nations. (2024). *Ad Hoc Committee on Cybercrime: Draft text of the comprehensive international convention*. https://www.unodc.org/unodc/en/cybercrime-ad_hoc_committee/ahc.html

Zetter, K. (2014). *Countdown to zero day: Stuxnet and the launch of the world's first digital weapon*. Crown.

6 Techplomacy

This chapter will argue that the major technology and internet companies are becoming so powerful that they now act like geopolitical actors in their own right. This has implications both for how governments deal with them and how these companies themselves develop their diplomatic capabilities. It first is worth defining what is meant by technology and internet companies. These include:

- Companies designing and producing digital hardware like Apple and Huawei
- Companies designing and producing digital software like Microsoft
- Major e-commerce companies like Amazon and Alibaba
- Search engines like Google and Baidu
- Digital and AI research conglomerates like Alphabet and Tencent
- Social media platforms like Meta/Facebook and Weibo
- Cybersecurity companies like Norton, Kaspersky and 360

Some of these companies operate in more than one category, and Google is of course a subsidiary of Alphabet. But this list identifies the kind of companies we will be discussing in this chapter.

Given the growing dependence of modern societies on digital technologies, the major technology and internet companies shape the geopolitical environment in the way that the major oil companies did in the past. Indeed, the power and economic muscle of the major internet companies parallels that of an oil company like Standard Oil at the beginning of the 20th century. The U.S. government responded to the economic and geopolitical influence this gave Standard Oil by using antitrust legislation to break it up. Although both the U.S. government and the European Commission have used anti-competition legislation against companies like Microsoft and Apple, they have not yet taken a drastic action against major internet companies. Conversely, the Chinese government has forced Alibaba to split its financial services from its e-commerce business.

DOI: 10.4324/9781032625089-7

As is clear from the list of internet companies above, the vast majority of major internet companies are concentrated in only two countries, China and the United States. These companies include leaders in hardware and software design, social media platforms, search engines, online retailers, mobile communications technologies, and AI applications. In part, this results from China's decision to limit, and in some cases block, the access of U.S. internet companies, and in particular U.S. social media platforms and search engines, to the Chinese market. This created the space in which domestic versions of the U.S. companies could emerge and thrive with the encouragement of the Chinese government. The EU, reflecting its regulatory geopolitical culture, preferred to try to regulate the activities of U.S. internet companies while allowing them to operate. The sheer size of the U.S. internet companies and the consequent economies of scale meant that there was little chance of domestic rivals emerging, apart from companies like Siemens, Nokia, and Ericsson, all of which are limited in scale and have trouble competing with United States and, increasingly, Chinese rivals. Efforts by the European Commission to talent spot and fund potential European internet giants of the future have so far proved unsuccessful. This concentration of internet companies in two countries does not only have economic consequences. To some extent, it shapes the geopolitical environment of the 21st century as well.

This provides second and third themes for techplomacy: how internet companies become geopolitical actors in their own right, and what this means for diplomacy and in particular how countries can develop ways of engaging with internet companies. In debates about internet governance, both China and the United States have an interest in protecting and promoting the interests of their companies, potentially distorting the debates. The technology and internet companies themselves are participating in these debates. They are not the only non-state actors, but their size and centrality to the digital economy make them particularly influential voices. Without significant internet companies of their own, regions like Europe lose influence. Moreover, whenever the EU seeks to regulate key internet-related sectors, for example regulating the use that social media platforms make of their users' data, they are in effect only regulating U.S. companies (the activities of Chinese social media platforms are essentially domestic). The U.S. government tends to see this as discrimination against U.S. companies, resulting in an increase in tensions between Washington and Brussels (Court of Justice of the European Union, 2024). Moreover, as we shall see, the internet companies themselves, intentionally or not, are increasingly behaving like geopolitical actors in their own right. Without finding ways of engaging with internet companies directly, governments (and the European Commission) find themselves even more marginalized in the key debates surrounding new technologies.

Despite growing geopolitical tensions, the major powers prefer to avoid direct conflict among themselves. The Russian invasion of Ukraine may appear to give the lie to this. But prior to the invasion, Russia did not regard Ukraine as a major power and specifically referred to the invasion as a special military action rather than war. In fact, the way in which the United States and other NATO countries have determinedly sought to avoid direct conflict with Russia, while providing Ukraine with military equipment and training, reinforces the point. Major powers seek to avoid direct military conflict in part because of the uncertainty involved (a hard lesson that Russia is learning in Ukraine) and in part of the risks of escalation, including to the level of using nuclear weapons. They therefore look for other non-military battlefields on which to play out their rivalry with less risks of escalation, or at least where the escalatory ladder is easier to control. Such alternative non-military battlefields can include trade, finance, and information. Even migrants can be weaponized to impose non-military coercion on other countries.

Given the importance of digital technologies and the internet to modern society, it was perhaps inevitable that geopolitical conflict would spread to the technology and internet sectors. Major powers seek to demonstrate their superiority through their domination of digital and associated technologies. As long ago as 2017, President Putin affirmed that 'whoever becomes the leader in this sphere (AI) will become the ruler of the world' (Quartz, 2017). Technological prowess becomes a measure of a country's geopolitical power, both symbolically and to the extent that it reinforces the country's economic, military, and cyber capabilities. The Biden administration sought to encourage the domestic technology sector (e.g. promoting the domestic production of computer chips through the so-called 'Chip Act') while banning the sale of chips and other sensitive components to China. In turn, China, through its 'made in China by 2025', seeks to be self-sufficient in key technologies. Increasingly states use the technologies on which cyberspace and the internet are constructed and the technology and internet companies which develop them in pursuit of wider geopolitical objectives (Bureau of Industry and Security, 2022).

The roll-out of the 5G networks for mobile telecommunications and, in particular, the role of the Chinese company Huawei in that roll-out provide an example of how technology and technology companies can become involved in geopolitical rivalries and the potential dangers for the global technological environment. The media controversy has centred around security concerns and the company's relationship with the Chinese government and security services. The U.S. government has argued that Huawei's role in the construction of the mobile network infrastructure for 5G, and associated cloud and other associated smart technologies, will give it access to sensitive data which it will share with the Chinese government. In support of this argument, the United States points out that the founder and CEO of Huawei, Ren Zhengfei, had served in the People's Liberation Army (PLA). On this basis, the U.S. government launched a campaign, with some success, to persuade its allies to exclude Huawei technology from their 5G mobile network infrastructure. In a possible related move, it sought the extradition of Ren's daughter, and Huawei CFO, from Canada on sanctions busting charges. Meng's subsequent detention in Canada provoked a diplomatic row between Canada and China with the retaliatory detention of Canadian citizens in China.

However, there may be a more interesting and significant long-term reason for the U.S. objection to Huawei than security. After all, Huawei technology already exists in the mobile network technology for 3G and 4G and remains there (mobile network infrastructures are built on top of each other). This relates to international industrial standards. International industrial standards ensure the international compatibility of new technologies allowing, for example, a mobile phone built and operated in Europe to function in China (and avoiding the problems of regionally incompatible DVDs and DVD readers). This is not simply a matter of convenience but essential to global economic efficiency and productivity. Traditionally, international industry standards for new stages of telecommunications technologies have been set by U.S. companies or companies based in U.S. allies like Japan or South Korea. The meetings for setting international industrial standards are not geopolitically events and attended mainly by technicians and industry representatives. Government representatives tend to be from technology- or industry-related ministries rather than the foreign ministry or intelligence services.

5G technologies allow much faster communication over mobile telecommunications networks (reduced latency) and much wider bandwidth. This is essential to the Internet of Things (IoT) which links not only human internet users but also a wide range of devices, ranging from domestic appliances to cars and industrial equipment (potentially the even wider bandwidth and reduced latency of 6G will be essential to the development of the Metaverse). Huawei has provided equipment and components for previous phases of mobile telephony (3G and 4G) but always as a manufacturer of equipment and components compliant with the standards set by others. The second phase of 5G, relevant to the interconnection of devices in the Internet of Things (IoT), is the first time that significant industry standards for a new technology have been set by a company based in a U.S. rival, namely Huawei in China. This threatens the previous hegemony of the United States and its allies in technological standards setting. International industry standards meetings, previously rather dull events for technicians, will become new battlefields for geopolitical influence. Foreign ministry officials and intelligence officers will join the technicians.

One of the keys to the geopolitical role of search engines and social media platforms in cyberspace are the algorithms that underlie them. The algorithms play different roles, but in both categories they shape the geography of cyberspace for certain activities, both in the sense of deciding what data arrives where and in placing limits on the reach of individual actors. In the case of search engines like Google, the algorithms decide in what order the results of an individual search are presented to the user. Given that most users do not look beyond the first page of Google results, this is important if a web content designer wants to secure high profile for their content. By studying how

Google operates, it is possible to identify key criteria which decide which webpages will get priority in a search. These are known as Search Engine Optimization (SEO) techniques. They are invaluable for e-commerce companies, journalists, or politicians who want to ensure that their web content secures profile and makes an impact (you can of course buy advertising which ensures priority as well, but the indication that your content is an advert undermines its credibility).

But bad actors can use the same SEO techniques to ensure that profile is given in searches to disinformation or provocative content. For example in late 2016, a search in Google for 'Did the holocaust happen?' generated a series of webpages by holocaust denial and neo-Nazi groups. The groups had studied Google's algorithms and manipulated them to secure priority for their holocaust denial material. It took Google some time to take down the holocaust denial sites, in part because it was reluctant to alter its search algorithms (or give away too many secrets about them) (Levin, 2016). This case may have produced more embarrassment than real damage, but it demonstrates the scope for malicious actors to use search engines to give profile to disinformation in an attempt to distort public debate and destabilize democratic societies. The danger is even greater with the development of 'Deepfake' techniques, in which a combination of machine learning and video techniques is used to generate videos in which people appear credibly to be saying things that they have not said (and would not say). While these techniques are still at an early stage of development, and some of the fake videos produced relatively easy to spot, they are improving rapidly. The dangers are not hard to foresee. The UAE-orchestrated hack of Qatar Government systems in 2017 resulted in the posting of inflammatory comments attributed to the Emir of Qatar. These 'fake statements' were sufficient to justify a Saudi-led blockade of Qatar (and secure the support of President Trump) (Nakashima & Entous, 2017). Had the UAE-orchestrated hackers been able also to post a 'deepfake' video of the Emir apparently making the statements in person, the impact would have been even more immediate and potentially more dangerous. The danger of deepfake videos is enhanced by video-sharing platforms like YouTube and Vimeo. The speed with which these platforms spread content means that the damage can be done before the victims of the deepfake can mitigate the consequences. Imagine, for example, the consequences of a deepfake video of a company's CEO apparently confessing that the company's data are unreliable. The speed of the circulation on video-sharing platforms would damage the company's share value long before the company had realized what was happening and issued a corrective. The scope for financial market fraud would be considerable. Technologies are being developed to identify deepfake videos, but they require time that the victims do not have. Another feature of video-sharing platforms are the underlying algorithms ensuring that users receive content they will like (we will explore these algorithms further below in the context of social media platforms). They will also ensure that deepfakes will be directed to those users pre-disposed to believe them, further complicating the task of those seeking to mitigate their effects (Chesney & Citron, 2019).

Algorithms function differently in social media platforms. There they aim at ensuring that the user receives content that he or she is likely to enjoy, be pleased with or interested in. Initially, this begins by suggesting contacts or friends who are likely to appeal to the user, to help him or her extend their social network. It then extends to content, and most importantly, to adverts tailored to the interests or tastes of the user. This essentially is how the social media plat forms are able to finance themselves. However, the problem is that the same algorithms that drive the tailored marketing also ensure that the user only receives the news and opinions that he or she is likely to like or agree with. Social media did not create the echo chambers which are undermining social and political narratives in Western societies, but they are reinforcing them. More seriously, like search engines, they can be used to spread disinformation and fake news, in efforts to influence and undermine Western political debates.

In a sense, the role of social media algorithms is even more pernicious than that of search engines. The algorithms underlying social media do not only spread disinformation. They also ensure that it arrives in the echo chambers most likely to be believed, where it fits in with the pre-existing prejudices of the members of the echo chamber.

Social media companies have proved reluctant to take these issues seriously. They have appointed hundreds of monitors to identify unacceptable content and remove it. Likewise, they use algorithms to identify 'bad actors' which they can ban from their platforms. But these actions are taken very much after the event and after the damage has been done. In part, this reflects the commercial requirement to protect their proprietary algorithms which ensure their incomes. They are reluctant to share these with governments. Partly, it reflects the way internet companies, especially Western internet companies, see themselves. This in turn reflects their experience of the internet (what critical geopolitics refers to as their 'geopolitical condition'). The internet already existed before the creation of internet companies. They were not instrumental in creating the internet, but nor did they experience it as a foreign imposition or an existential threat. Rather, it was something in which they developed, and without which they could not exist. Above all it was a commercial opportunity.

Since their invention, both search engines and social media platforms have gone through various phases. The first phase is what might be called the idealistic phase, captured by Google's motto 'Don't be evil' (subsequently adapted during Google's restructuring as Alphabet to 'Do the right thing'). The internet companies saw themselves as new kinds of entities pursuing moral paths, as forces for good in the world. As they became ever wealthier, the moral aspects were undermined. Google's initial refusal to collaborate with Chinese government censorship had broken down by 2018, as it agreed to develop a special search machine for China (to the consternation of many of its own workers who appear to have forced Google to abandon the Dragonfly project at the end of 2018). Facebook found itself caught up in a series of scandals about the use it allowed to be made of its users' data. The Cambridge Analytica scandal revealed that Facebook had allowed Cambridge Analytica to use applications to gather Facebook users' data to allow more targeted campaigning in the U.S. elections. Particularly controversial was a questionnaire that Cambridge Analytica developed which allowed the company access to the data not only of users who filled in the questionnaire but also of all their 'friends' on Facebook. These problems and scandals marked a second phase in the internet companies' experience of cyberspace, where they moved from being forces for good to being seen by the public, and reluctantly by themselves, as mechanisms for monetizing the data of their users. This provoked growing concerns among the public and government, in particular in western Europe, about the use and protection of citizens' data. As noted in previously, this culminated in the European Commission developing the GDPR to protect the data of European citizens (European Commission, 2016). However, the internet companies are still unwilling, or unable, to accept or assimilate the third phase of their experience of cyberspace: as active players in geopolitical conflict in cyberspace.

Three concepts from critical geopolitics can help us analyse the position of internet companies in cyberspace. Geopolitical culture describes the way a country sees itself in relation to the geopolitical environment and the way it thinks about engagement with other international actors. It depends in part on a country's political country and partly on its perception of its own history. As we have seen, the geopolitical condition describes how a country has experienced new technologies, in the case of digital technologies. Finally, geopolitical fields describe the different policy and physical spaces in which a country operates. For internet companies, the geopolitical condition is the experience of digital technologies not only as something normal but also as essential to their own existence. The geopolitical field in which they operate initially centred on information gathering or building social networks, but increasingly this is fragmenting into different geopolitical fields describing their interactions with users, advertisers, governments, and each other. Their objectives and behaviour in each of these fields can vary dramatically. Unlike states, they do not have a geopolitical culture that precedes, or is separate from, their engagement with cyberspace. Their geopolitical culture derives from their engagement with cyberspace. Thus, deriving from their initial geopolitical field, spreading information, and promoting social interaction online, it is positive, seeing them as almost altruistic operators in cyberspace. Only slowly as the geopolitical fields in which they operated shifted to commercial marketing and the monetizing of their users' data did their geopolitical culture have to accept the commercial element, but still along-side their self-image as a force for good. They still have not been able to assimilate the implications of the final geopolitical field in which they operate, the battlefield for information conflict between, primarily, Russia and the West. From the point of view of geopolitical culture, they remain in denial (perhaps analogous to the kind of self-denial generated by U.S. exceptionalism).

It may be worth mentioning here Zuboff's work (2019) on surveillance capitalism. Zuboff's thesis is that internet companies discovered that they were gathering a lot of 'waste data' about their users, data that they did not need to improve the services being offered to their users. They realized that this data could be processed to construct profiles of their users which could be sold to advertisers in pursuit of the advertising grail of targeted advertising. This was supported by the algorithms we have already discussed. The key was to minimize the uncertainty in the behaviour of their users to the benefit of the advertising customers by detailed profiles of users to which advertising could be directed. This became the business model of search engines as well social media platforms. But it is not simply a question of the data which users consciously upload onto these platforms. With the advent of smartphones, enormous quantities of data can be collected and processed without the awareness of the users. In an amusing example, data collected and published by a running app identified the location of American military bases. Google will even process how users of its search engines misspell their searches in building up their profiles. This in effect undermines the effectiveness of the GDPR. Zuboff argues that companies like Google and Facebook now wish to take this a stage further by using these profiles not just to predict their users' behaviour more accurately but also to shape that behaviour by providing constant and targeted prompts to their users. At the relatively innocent level, this would amount to reminding a user about their love of strawberry doughnuts when passing a store selling strawberry doughnuts. But it is not hard to see how this use of profiles for targeted prompting of users' behaviour could have more dystopian interpretations. At the very least, it gives an indication of the power that these companies acquire through their access to vast quantities of data and the capacity to process and reinforces the suggestion that they should be treated as more than just commercial companies.

The wider activities of Facebook's parent company Meta make even clearer the extent to which it has become a geopolitical actor, whether or not it admits it to itself. We have already noted how Facebook, as it then was, planned to issue its own digital currency based on a basket of currencies and assets (Diem Association, 2020). The aim was to generate a currency linked to the Facebook platform which would allow anyone in the world to be able to trade internationally without the need to access U.S. dollars or a bank account. The basket of currencies and assets would be chosen by Facebook and would make the new digital currency independent of any given physical fiat currency. Zuckerberg did not hide his ambition to replace the U.S. dollar for many online transactions. The creation of such a currency would have been a deeply geopolitical act with implications which Facebook itself seemed to have underestimated. Apart from the dangers of money laundering and other illegal activities taking advantage of a currency unregulated by any central bank, a global digital currency of the kind to which Facebook appeared to aspire threatened to undermine the international reserve currency status of the U.S. dollar. This reserve currency status of the dollar affords the United States significant geopolitical advantages. First, it enables the United States to run fiscal deficits that would be unsustainable for other countries. But possibly more significant, it also allows the United States to impose unilateral sanctions on countries, backed up by secondary sanctions on companies which then breach those sanctions. It is able to do so because the dollar remains the international currency of trade, and companies need to be able to trade in dollars, making them vulnerable to secondary sanctions. Zuckerberg appears not to have appreciated the geopolitical significance of launching an international digital currency or anticipate the backlash from the U.S. Congress and the U.S. Federal Reserve. Various sponsors, unnerved by the backlash, pulled out. The proposal has now been reduced to a digital currency based on the dollar (and therefore no threat to the global reserve status of the dollar) for use by Facebook users. Even in this modest form, it has not yet emerged.

Mark Zuckerberg reinforced this sense of Facebook/Meta as a geopolitical actor when he announced Facebook's commitment to the creation of the Metaverse and in particular Facebook's investment in the Augmented Reality (AR) and Virtual Reality (VR) technology, where glasses or headsets are necessary to access it. This commitment to developing the Metaverse was symbolized by his decision to change the name of Facebook's holding company to Meta. Meta is not the only company gambling on the development of the Metaverse. Tim Sweeney, CEO of online gaming platform Epic games, has 'had Metaverse ambitions for a long time'. Sony and Microsoft are also committed to its development. Some commentators have argued that the Metaverse is the next logical stage in the evolution of internet. The internet has evolved from the phase of early modem connections through personal computers and laptops to the current mobile networking phase. Our current level of online interconnectedness through smartphones and the devices of the Internet of Things would have been inconceivable during earlier phases of the internet, even at the time of the introduction of the first iPhone. The level of online interconnectedness of younger people, whether communicating with each other through online messaging apps or through online gaming platforms, has even led some commentators to suggest that many people already live in a primitive version of the Metaverse.

Metaverse commentator Matthew Ball (2022) defines the Metaverse as:

> A massively scaled and interoperable network of real-time rendered 3D virtual worlds that can be experienced synchronously and persistently by an effective unlimited number of users with an individual sense of presence, and with continuity of data, such as identity, history, entitlements, objects, communications and payments.

This is an ambitious description in which the Metaverse performs like a genuinely parallel world with the main difference being that we can choose our own avatars to express ourselves as we would like to appear rather than as we are. An idea of what this world might be like can be seen in Neal Stephenson's dystopian novel *Snow Crash*. But it requires that large numbers of people can have real-time access, that the identity of avatars is stable throughout time, that past events are remembered in the system as are entitlements (in the sense of qualities, properties, or property that avatars collect), that avatars and their entitlements can move between different parts of the Metaverse (interoperability), and that 3D events can be rendered in real time. These pose significant challenges which the existing technology cannot solve. Particular problems include the lack of computing power, high network latency and limited bandwidth, and low-quality VR and AR equipment. Zuckerberg admits that one of the great challenges will be providing sufficient computing power in headsets which nevertheless remain wearable. Meta's proposal of including more sensors in its VR devices to ensure that avatars reflect users' real-life expressions raises significant data protection and privacy issues (Zuckerberg does not have a good record on either). Indeed, issues related to data protection, privacy, and inline governance promise to be even more difficult in the Metaverse than they are in cyberspace.

Significant questions remain about the Metaverse, even if the technological issues can be resolved. These include:

- Will it be constructed top-down by corporations like Meta, Microsoft, or Google, or will it evolve bottom up from the progressive combination of smaller Virtual Reality worlds and gaming platforms?
- What role will governments play in the development of the Metaverse?
- Crucially, will there be a single Metaverse, albeit a network of smaller Virtual Reality worlds, or multiple metaverses in competition or even conflict with each other?

The construction of the Metaverse implies significant challenges for diplomacy. The Metaverse will not arise as a unitary fait accompli in a world where U.S. hegemony is sufficient to minimize state opposition like the internet. It will be geopolitically challenged from the beginning. The European Union is already wondering how to regulate it. Authoritarian governments have a vested interest in establishing sovereignty rights and undermining a single Metaverse which might threaten regime stability. Internet and gaming corporations will need to negotiate among themselves and with governments on the terms and protocols for the creation of the Metaverse. This may cause a demand in the corporate sector for the kind of negotiating and networking skills in which diplomats specialize. It remains to be seen whether they seek to meet these needs by recruiting diplomats, and what strain these place on governments' diplomatic resources (we will see later how Microsoft was able to outbid the Danish Foreign Ministry for the services of its Tech Ambassador).

Once the Metaverse is constructed, it will need rules, protocols, and norms of behaviour if it is not to become a Hobbesian world of all against all. Leaving this to the corporate builders of the Metaverse risks a loss of democratic legitimacy and accountability. Many advocates of the Metaverse, like many original advocates of the internet, are sceptical of government involvement and would like to see the Metaverse free from government interference. This has not proved possible with the internet, and it seems unlikely that some form of government involvement in the Metaverse will be avoided either. If the concept of sovereignty is not established in the Metaverse, it may make little sense having virtual embassies there other than for public diplomacy and national marketing. There is general agreement that a thriving digital economy will be essential for the sustainability of the Metaverse, probably backed by cryptocurrencies, non-fungible tokens (NFTs), and blockchain technology. But this raises the questions of who will enforce contracts and guarantee property rights (the essential roles of governments in real-world economies): governments, a new Metaverse governance body (in which case who will belong and how will they be chosen?), or decentralized blockchain technologies (as the libertarian supporters of the Metaverse advocate)?

The issue of terrorism illustrates how a real-world phenomenon could infect the Metaverse and require a diplomatic response. The Metaverse will inevitably be a tempting target for terrorists and terrorist groups (as it will be for organized crime). How terrorists might take advantage of the Metaverse is suggested by terrorist activity in cyberspace. In spite of the fears about cyberterrorism, there is limited, if any, evidence of any groups trying to carry out direct terrorist attacks via cyberspace (although one might argue that some of the activities of state-backed non-state actors in cyberspace get close to terrorism). There may be many reasons for this. One will be the technical difficulty of carrying out a cyberattack that has the same visual impact of planting a bomb. In general, terrorist groups have preferred to use cyberspace for raising funds (whether through donations or criminal activities), communications, recruitment, and propaganda.

Terrorist activity in the Metaverse may depend on whether there is a single Metaverse or competing metaverses. Cyberterrorism may be more attractive in a single Metaverse. It depends on the socio-economic importance of the Metaverse in society and the psychological dependency it engenders among its users. Terrorists or motivated groups of activists could carry our cyberattacks to delay or disrupt the construction of the Metaverse. Disinformation operations could sow dissent among the various actors in the construction. In this, they could receive support from state actors suspicious of the creation of the Metaverse. Once the Metaverse is created, they could launch cyberattacks against individual avatars or groups of avatars or destroy or damage symbolic virtual institutions. This could cause economic or psychological damage with low risk for the terrorists. Their ability to raise funds donations, selling non-fungible tokens (NFTs), or scams and other criminal activities would be facilitated by the expected reliance of the Metaverse on cryptocurrencies.

Multiple metaverses in competition or conflict would create similar opportunities for terrorist groups. But it would also offer them the chance to create their own metaverses driven by their own ideologies. These could be used for communication, propaganda, and financing. But even more dangerous would be to attract young people to play out their fantasies in an unattributed terrorist metaverse as a first step into recruiting them for terrorist activities. Monitoring each metaverse in a world of multiple competing metaverses will be a major challenge for security forces.

The internet took diplomats by surprise. They were slow to understand that not all problems in cyberspace were technical ones that could be left to technicians. Only relatively recently have they realized that the most pressing of problems in cyberspace are political and geopolitical and need diplomatic management. The Metaverse has been long advertised. The diplomats have no excuse not to start thinking how to engage with it. They, and their governments, must seize the opportunity to shape it. Governments must decide what kind of Metaverse they want to see and the norms and rules underlying its construction and operation. Above all, they must seek international cooperation to limit the scope of action of terrorists whether in a single Metaverse or multiple metaverses. This will require an effective multistakeholder diplomacy in which diplomats can engage effectively with a range of non-state actors from internet companies and gaming platforms to users and activist groups. It also requires a diplomacy based on interests rather than values and ideology. An effective diplomacy to limit the activities of terrorists in the Metaverse cannot exclude major and influential countries because we disagree with their values or ideologies.

The reason for this discursion into the Metaverse is twofold. First, it shows yet again how the major internet companies are straying from the purely commercial into areas more appropriate to state actors. The effort to develop a global virtual world parallel to the real world is undoubtedly a political if not geopolitical act. Its implications are highly geopolitical, as are the controversies it is likely to cause. Second, it again demonstrates the need for diplomats and diplomacy to engage with technology and internet and technology companies, not just as commercial operators but as fellow geopolitical actors. In the last chapter, we discussed the geopolitics of cyberspace, and how this conditions the engagement of state and non-state actors in cyberspace. The geopolitics of cyberspace is still at a very early stage and still needs much work. But analysts and diplomats already need to start reflecting on the geopolitics of the Metaverse.

There is another sector of technology and internet companies with clear geopolitical implications: private cybersecurity companies (PCCs). At the moment, PCCs focus on offering passive cyber defence for their clients and cyberattack attribution, produced by their cyber forensic capabilities (the technical analysis and tracking back of cyberattacks to their origins). Most PCCs allow their staff 10% of their time for 'research', much of which is devoted to honing their skills in cyber forensics. The cyber defence and cyber forensic capabilities of these companies exceed that of most governments. Their offer of passive cyber defence services to both governments and companies is relatively uncontroversial. Their publication of cyberattack attributions is more complicated. Although some attributions are for clients, in other cases, PCCs publish attributions for marketing reasons. In the case of a severe cyberattack, possibly even causing physical (kinetic) damage or loss of life, the victim government would come under pressure to respond. It may not want to publish an early attribution, either because it is not sufficiently confident in the attribution or because it does not want to publish the attribution until it has decided how to respond. PCCs are unconcerned about such considerations. But if the PCC publishes its attribution for marketing reasons, it puts the government under enormous pressure to act. The result can be unnecessary escalation of response or even a new cyberconflict if the attribution is wrong (the 2015 WannaCry ransomware attack was originally attributed to Russian hackers. The attribution was subsequently changed to North Korean hackers).

The position becomes more critical if PCCs develop the capacity for offensive cyber operations and offer these services to governments. There is also considerable debate about active defence measures in cybersecurity, where the hacker himself is hacked to prevent further attacks. Most governments prohibit private companies from doing this, although it is an effective form of cyber defence, because it seems to close cyber vigilantes. Governments try to retain the monopoly on legitimate 'violence in cyberspace'. But with the majority of governments lacking the offensive cyber capabilities which PCCs are able to develop, it seems inevitable that at some point, PCCs will offer these 'cyber mercenary' services to governments (and possibly also companies). To some extent this already happens. In the United States, federal pay scales restrict how much government cyber agencies like the National Security Agency can pay their cyber technicians. This means that they frequently lose out in recruiting the brightest technicians to the private sector. They get round this by using contractors who are not bound by federal wage scales and rules. These contractors frequently are involved in offensive operations. Edward Snowden was working for Booze Allen, not the NSA or CIA, when he leaked the documents about the U.S. cyber activities.

This use of contractors for offensive cyber operations raises similar questions to the use of Private Military Security Companies (PMSCs) like Blackwater as contractors in Iraq. The performance of Blackwater in Iraq demonstrated problems relating to chains of command, accountability, legal responsibility, and rules of procedure. Similar problems in principle could arise with PCCs operating as contractors for offensive cyber operations for governments which otherwise cannot attract the best qualified technicians (like the United States) or who lack the offensive capabilities themselves. Russia has not yet used PCCs for offensive cyber operations, preferring to use criminal cyber gangs when they wish to use surrogates for cyberattacks. But they have used a private company for disinformation operations and spreading fake news through social media platforms and the Internet Research Agency (ironically better known by its acronym IRA) and increasingly make geopolitical use of the private military security company Wagner. Apart from these examples, the dangers of cyber mercenary PCCs offering their services to governments for offensive operations appear to lie in the future, but it may be a very near future. Any effort to regulate the performance of PCCs at a global level will require an effective multilateral diplomacy, in which the interests of the EU and LAC countries should be aligned. It will also require an effective engagement with the PCCs themselves (Citizen Lab, 2024).

In 2017, Denmark appointed an ambassador to the high technology sector, commonly known as Denmark's Tech Ambassador (Denmark Ministry of Foreign Affairs, 2024). France and Germany followed suit in 2018. However, the French Ambassador appears to be mainly concerned with preventing the use of social media and search machines to promote terrorism. Following a meeting with the German Envoy for Technology and Digitalization, Denmark's first Tech Ambassador Caspar Klynge tweeted that there was significant overlap between their roles, but it is not clear what this is. The German Envoy is not an ambassador to the technology sector as such, and his role seems more ambiguous and less innovative. Other nations have envoys responsible for the technology sector or digital technologies, but they are not configured as ambassadors as such. The European External Action Service (EEAS) is apparently considering appointing its own Tech Ambassador.

The Office of Denmark's Tech Ambassador (as the Tech Embassy is officially called) was not originally limited to one physical site (as would be the case with a bilateral embassy), but split across three sights: Silicon Valley, Copenhagen, and Beijing. There is talk of opening a further office in East Africa. Denmark's first Tech Ambassador Klynge coined the term Techplomacy to refer to his role (and has launched a podcast 'Techplomacy' to explore and promote it further). He has described the key roles of his mission as:

- Gathering information on new and future technological developments and analysing their impact on diplomacy, politics, and Danish society
- Gathering information on developments within the technological sector itself, relations between tech companies, and their plans for future operations/investments
- Discussing ethical and regulatory issues with technological companies, with a focus on unacceptable content and data and privacy protection
- Convincing technology companies to base operations, research facilities, or European subsidiaries in Denmark
- Promoting Denmark as a highly digitalized country at the cutting edge of new technologies and thinking (Klynge's appointment as Denmark's Tech Ambassador itself contributes to this)

Klynge's description of his role raises several interesting issues. The different offices out of which he operates (Silicon Valley, Copenhagen, and Beijing) give a fair idea of where Denmark sees as centres of technological innovation in the 21st century, as do the plans for a further centre in East Africa. It is interesting that they have not situated an office in the EU (other than the office in Copenhagen, which effectively gives the Tech Ambassador a home base). But then it is also interesting that it is the Danish Foreign Ministry, rather than the European External Action Service, that has taken the initiative to set up a Mission to the Tech Sector.

Although Klynge proclaims a new kind of diplomacy, Techplomacy for his mission, his job description looks remarkably like that of a traditional Ambassador or Embassy: gathering and analysing information about the country in which he is stationed and its implications for his home country, engaging the host government in discussions about regulatory issues and international law (particularly relevant in EU countries), engaging with the commercial and financial sectors to attract Foreign Direct Investment (FDI), and the promotion of his own country. The only two key activities of traditional embassies missing are engaging with the host government on geopolitical issues (but see below) and consular protection. The latter may be implicit, however, in the discussion of ethical and regulatory issues – at least in part aimed at the protection of the rights of Danish citizens in cyberspace. It is not that the diplomacy is different, but that its target has changed, reflecting the development of cyberspace and the importance of technology companies. Indeed, Klynge's appointment recognizes the importance of technological developments, especially in digitalization, artificial intelligence, and machine learning, to the development of international relations, and to the physical and economic security of countries like Denmark. On the Mission to the Tech Sector's webpage, Klynge explicitly recognizes that 'Techplomacy' should be seen as complementary to traditional diplomacy.

Klynge sought to build multistakeholder platforms with the tech sector, and other groups or individuals interested in the key issues, which can support the effort of his colleagues working with governments and international organizations. The Mission also implicitly recognized internet and technological companies as geopolitical players in their own right, which are shaping the geopolitical environment in both physical and cyberspace and in which states have to operate. This is not the first time that private companies have shaped the geopolitical environment – it could be argued that both telecommunication and oil companies have done so in the past. But no country in the past has felt the need to create a mission and ambassador specifically to these sectors. Something has changed. Much of the work Klynge appeared to be doing initially (to judge from the Mission webpage and his Twitter feed) focused on public-diplomacy-like activities to engage not only with internet and technology companies but also with a wider public to promote an understanding of his mission. Thus, he participated in a series of conferences and workshops, including those at the UN General Assembly. But he has launched 'Ambassador for one Day', in which U.S. university students (interestingly, not Danish university students) could compete to spend one day replacing Klynge as Denmark's Tech Ambassador. These public diplomacy activities no doubt helped establish the standing and credibility of Denmark's Mission to the Tech Sector and, as such, contribute to the Mission objectives/job description (as set out above). However, there are other issues about how Klynge and his team relate to the tech sector and, in particular, internet companies (especially social media platforms and search engines).

The Danish government appointed a Tech Ambassador to develop Denmark's relationship with the tech sector, promote Denmark as a centre for technology innovation, and ensure that Denmark remains abreast of the latest technological developments. The role is also to engage in debates about technology regulation and issues such as data protection. But the world has moved on significantly since the appointment. The use of social media platforms in disinformation operations, the attempt by a social media platform to launch its own global currency, the debates about the involvement of technology companies with their governments, and the setting of international industrial standards have all reinforced the idea of technology companies as geopolitical actors in their own right, with the privileges and responsibilities that such actors enjoy. This suggests that the remit of the Tech Ambassador may have to expand to treat the tech sector as one would nation-states, and not always as friendly ones. However, the Danish government seems to have taken the opposite tack following Klynge's departure, reducing the Tech Ambassador to a more traditional tech envoy focused on the European Union (Reuters, 2022). The experiment ended.

Similar questions arise about the technology and internet companies themselves. If they are geopolitical actors, or are perceived as such, they need to develop their own techplomacy capacities. As shown by Facebook's clumsy launch of Libra/Diem, if you aspire to a role that others perceive as geopolitical, you need to develop a diplomatic approach or strategy, regardless of your self-perception as a commercial company. Likewise, technology companies navigating through the newly dangerous minefields of international industry standards meetings will need diplomacy as well as technical skills, not just to secure the right to set industrial standards in the first place but also to survive the geopolitical disputes of the subsequent technology roll-outs. Microsoft at least has recognized this and decided to appoint what is effectively a Microsoft ambassador to the EU. In a supreme irony, it recruited Klynge himself as the first occupant of the position (Microsoft, 2021).

The rapidly developing digital technology, internet, and AI sectors are throwing up a host of political and geopolitical problems requiring diplomatic management at the international level. Major powers are increasingly turning technology and the technology industries into new battlefields for their geopolitical rivalry. The major technological and internet companies increasingly appear like the oil companies of the 20th century as geopolitical actors in their own right. Managing these three issues requires governments to develop an effective techplomacy to engage not only with each other but also with the technology and internet companies themselves (these companies need to develop their techplomacy, as Facebook/Meta has learnt to its cost, although it is still not clear whether it has learnt the lesson as well as Microsoft).

References

Ball, M. (2022). *The metaverse: And how it will revolutionize everything*. W. W. Norton & Company.

Bureau of Industry and Security. (2022). *Summary of the October 7, 2022 semiconductor export controls*. U.S. Department of Commerce. https://www.bis.doc.gov/index.php/documents/about-bis/newsroom/press-releases/3158-2022-10-07-bis-press-release-advanced-computing-and-semiconductor-manufacturing-controls-final/file

Chesney, R., & Citron, D. K. (2019). Deep fakes: A looming challenge for privacy, democracy, and national security. *California Law Review, 107*(6), 1753–1819.

Citizen Lab. (2024). *Cyber mercenaries and the privatization of cyber power*. University of Toronto. https://citizenlab.ca

Court of Justice of the European Union. (2024, September 10). *Press release No 133/24: Commission v Ireland and others* (Apple). Curia. https://curia.europa.eu/jcms/upload/docs/application/pdf/2024-09/cp240133en.pdf

Denmark Ministry of Foreign Affairs. (2024, May 23). *Denmark seeks to strengthen European tech diplomacy and global engagement*. https://techamb.um.dk/blog/denmark-seeks-to-strengthen-european-tech-diplomacy-and-global-engagement/

Diem Association. (2020, December 1). *Announcing the Diem: A new name for the Libra project*. https://www.diem.com/en-us/updates/announcing-diem/

European Commission. (2016, May 4). Regulation (EU) 2016/679 (General data protection regulation). *Official Journal of the European Union, L 119*. https://eur-lex.europa.eu/eli/reg/2016/679/oj

Levin, S. (2016, December 20). *Google alters search results to remove Holocaust denial from top results* [News article]. The Guardian.

Microsoft. (2021, April 26). *Microsoft hires Denmark's first tech ambassador, Casper Klynge, as VP European government affairs* [Press release]. https://news.microsoft.com/europe/2021/04/26/microsoft-hires-denmarks-first-tech-ambassador-casper-klynge-as-vp-european-government-affairs/

Nakashima, E., & Entous, A. (2017, July 16). *UAE hacked Qatari government sites, sparking regional upheaval, according to U.S. intelligence officials*. The Washington Post. https://www.washingtonpost.com/world/national-security/uae-hacked-qatari-government-sites-sparking-regional-upheaval-according-to-us-intelligence-officials/2017/07/16/00c46e54-698f-11e7-8eb5-cbccc2e7bfbf_story.html

Quartz. (2017, September 1). *Putin: "Whoever becomes the leader in AI will rule the world"* [News article].

Reuters. (2022, June 6). *Denmark names new tech ambassador with narrower role* [News article].

Zuboff, S. (2019). *The age of surveillance capitalism*. Profile Books.

Conclusion

Leading with Diplomacy: Building Corporate Resilience in an Unpredictable World

A former Chinese trade official and a former British diplomat have come together to explore how companies can benefit from the insights and techniques of diplomacy in managing and mitigating geopolitical risk. This is a reversal of recent trends in two senses. First, the West and China have been moving towards confrontation rather than cooperation. Second, diplomats have repeatedly been told to learn from the private sector and import business management techniques into the running of diplomatic services and embassies. Unsurprisingly, we think both trends are profoundly mistaken.

Our thesis in this book is that there is a diplomatic approach to managing international relations, including both mindset and techniques, which can be adapted to help companies better manage the challenges of the international business environment. A sceptical reader might ask, if this diplomatic approach to international relations is so effective, why have governments not created a stable and predictable environment for international business. There are many answers to this question, which go well beyond the scope of this book. But in an earlier chapter, we refer to permacrisis – one crisis follows another – and policrisis – multiple crises hit at the same time. When these terms were created in the wake of COVID and the Russian invasion of Ukraine, they were used to denote a particularly dangerous and volatile world which presented governments with uniquely dangerous challenges. We forget our history. This panicked reaction to perma and policrises would have surprised statesmen of previous centuries who lived with both and assumed that they were natural features of the international environment. History in fact suggests that volatility and unpredictability are the natural state of the international environment and that the relative stability of the international rule-based order (either dated from 1945 or 1991) is the anomaly (and true for only limited regions of the world). This may explain why the diplomatic approach to international relations tends to focus on managing problems rather than solving them. As Kissinger is reported to have said, the tragedy of foreign policy is that too often all the options are bad: the task of the statesman is to nudge the world towards the least bad option (Gewen, 2020).

DOI: 10.4324/9781032625089-8

Our persistent sceptic may insist that if diplomats are so good at managing this volatile and unpredictable world, why should not companies delegate the management of geopolitical risk to their governments. After all, it is what they pay their taxes for. This time we have more specific answers for our sceptic. Companies should work closely with their governments and diplomats in managing geopolitical risk. But there are several reasons why companies should not depend on their governments. First, the interests of the company may not coincide with those of their government. The government must reflect the broad national interests of the state as a whole. Taking action on behalf of the company may damage more important national risks or put at risks the interests of other companies. In some cases, companies may even find greater support from the governments of other countries. For example European telecommunications companies seeking to overthrow the principle of net neutrality in the operating of the internet are likely to encounter more support from the U.S. government than their own. Second, a company's government may not have the relevant influence to be able to help the company. Not all governments are equally influential with other countries or their governments. Alternately, the diplomats may be too far away from where the company is encountering problems and not enjoy the networks of influence at the level. Where a company is operating far from the national capital, their own networks are likely to be richer and more effective than the distant embassy. Finally, a company's government may be part of the problem. The measures being taken against the company, or the problems the company is encountering, may reflect broader tensions between the company's own government and that of the country where it is working. In such circumstances, the company may not want to advertise its nationality or find it more effective to find other allies.

It may be worth at this point to say a word about geopolitical risk. The term geopolitical risk is used throughout the book and is in common usage. Geopolitical risk companies offer consultancy services to companies, both in terms of analysis and strategy. And yet there has been relatively little effort to define what 'geopolitics' means. Often, the term simply seems to be a way of talking about a more realist, almost realpolitik, approach to international relations. On other occasions, it is used to imply that geography in some sense defines, or at least constrains, political relations between states (Kaplan, 2012). Indeed, one of the reasons for the absence of geopolitics as a subject from most Western universities following the Second World War was a concern about this apparent geographical determinism (the other reason was the close association between German geopoliticians like Haushofer and the Nazi party; Murphy, 1997). For our purposes, we recast 'geopolitics' as the political meaning or interpretation of geography. This reflects the idea that while geography (generally speaking) does not change, its political meaning can and does. One example will suffice. During the Cold War, NATO strategists were obsessed about the Fulda Gap, on the border of East and

West Germany, through which they were convinced that a Soviet armoured attack on the West would flow. Now Fulda is a sleepy town in the middle of a united Germany. By contrast, during the Cold War, the Suwalki Gap was an irrelevant stretch of territory between Warsaw Pact Poland and Soviet Republic Lithuania. Now it is a potential corridor between Belarus and the Russian enclave Kaliningrad which would cut off NATO allies Poland and Lithuania. NATO's strategists are again interested. The geography remains the same, the political interpretation changes. If geopolitics is the political meaning or interpretation of geography, then geopolitical risk consists in the risks that changes in the political meaning or interpretation can generate. In the 21st century, changes in political interpretation affect an increasingly broad range of areas, including trade, information, finance, technology, and cyber, as geopolitical conflicts are fought out by non-military means.

Chapter 3 of this book stresses the importance of company-centred analysis of geopolitical risk. Each industrial or commercial sector faces its own sector-specific range of geopolitical risks. Each company within a given sector has its own company culture and risk tolerance. Some companies are willing to take risks that others are not. For example the family-owned machine tool company horrified when it accidentally breaches a dual use sanctions regime versus the company that repeatedly breaches such regimes, considering the risk worth the premium it can charge for its products. Finally, geography also matters (well it would, wouldn't it). A company's geopolitical risk profile will depend on its geopolitical distribution. The risk it runs in one market will depend on in which other markets it is also present. It needs to understand if investing in new markets will hedge against risks in other markets or double down on the existing risks. The analysis must start with the company and work out. Failure to take account of these nuances results in the kind of generic geopolitical risk reports peddled by geopolitical risk consultancies to unsuspecting clients. Company-centred analysis is also relevant to cyber risks. As indicated in Chapter 6, the risks of cyberattacks on companies are increasing exponentially. As this chapter is being written, the British government is considering what support it can give to the component makers for the car company Jaguar Land Rover, whose operations have been frozen by a cyberattack. Of particular concern has been the growth of ransomware attacks, whereby hackers freeze a company's data until the company pays a cryptocurrency payment to secure its release (Smeets, 2025). Hackers are also now stealing sensitive data which they threaten to release if the company is slow in paying the ransom. Ransomware attacks are typically carried out by organized criminal gangs, but the distinction between criminal and political cyberattacks is often ambiguous. Some governments will tolerate criminal cyberattacks if they also serve their purposes. Other governments will actively collaborate with criminal cyber gangs. In the case of North Korea, cybercrime is carried out as a state policy to raise funds for the regime. Company-centred analysis is crucial to defending against such threats. Key questions include: What sensitive information do I hold within my systems? Who would be interested in it? How much would it be worth to them? What would they want to do with it? What are my greatest vulnerabilities (technical or human)? Answering these questions helps understand what kinds of hackers are most likely to attack you. It also helps understand the level and kind of technical defences needed and devising mitigation strategies for when the attack strikes.

The book discusses the difficulties of managing global supply chains, brought home to many companies both by COVID and the Russian invasion of Ukraine. A key skill which can contribute to SCM is socialization. This is relevant to companies' cybersecurity too because, as Chapter 6 argues, cyber vulnerabilities often lie not in the headquarters company but further down the supply chain. Supply chain participants in other countries may not be working within the same regulatory or legislative frameworks (this can be a major problem with treatment of workers, for example). They may not take rigorous steps in cybersecurity. The role of socialization in diplomacy has been discussed by Sharp (2009) in the context of the irruption of revolutionary states into the international system. Revolutionary regimes initially do not play by the international rules. Soviet embassies in the early 1920s, for example, aimed not to manage the Soviet Union's relations with other countries, but to serve as centres to promote the worldwide revolution, including containing significant numbers of weapons. By the 1930s, Ivan Maisky as Soviet ambassador in London could scarcely be distinguished from his fellow ambassadors, apart from, perhaps, his even more extensive and effective contact networks (Gorodetsky, 2015). This socialization of would-be revolutionaries into the international community of diplomats was repeated with Chinese diplomats following the Cultural Revolution, Iranian diplomats following the Iranian revolution, and Libyan diplomats during the regime of Qadaffi. In each case, the revolutionaries are socialized into behaving according to the rules and norms of traditional diplomacy. The lesson for companies with international supply chains is the need to socialize the different participants in the supply chain so that they share the culture and norms of the headquarter company. Even if they operate in countries with very different regulatory and legislative frameworks, the norms they internalize through the socialization process will lead them to ways that support the operations of the headquarters company. For example the internalising of norms relating cyber security will improve the security of the systems they operate, even if this does not form part of the cultural or regulatory environment in which they operate.

If we do live in a permacrisis, as we have suggested, then management becomes crisis management. Companies need to change the way they think about planning and strategy. Publishing two-year strategic plans may keep financial market analysts happy and bump up the share price, but they make little sense if the geopolitical environment, and thus the international business environment, can change dramatically in that time frame. In the world of diplomacy, a strategic plan is an oxymoron. There is planning and there is strategy, and the two are different. As Eisenhower pointed out, the plan is nothing, the planning is everything. Another of Kissinger's bon mots was that the problem with foreign policy was that when you have greatest freedom of action, you have least information. But if you wait for more information, you lose your freedom of action. Time (and other actors) close down your options. Business school teaching of strategic planning is taking more account of uncertainty and imperfect knowledge, but it still does not take account of the radical uncertainty of the world of perma and policrises. Nor does it take sufficient account of the old military say 'the other guy always gets a vote'. Too often, it feels like playing chess with oneself. What Eisenhower meant was that the plan would soon become irrelevant as soon as the fighting began (or as Moltke put it, no plan survives first contact with the enemy), but that the exercise of planning put officers in a much better position to react to changes in the external environment and to adapt to changes to the plan. We cannot predict the future (any geopolitical analyst who claims to be able to do so is a charlatan), but thinking about possible futures and what they might mean for our company can better prepare us for what the world throws at us. Scenario building and other modelling techniques that let us explore possible future worlds reinforce our ability to develop strategies built on flexibility and adaptability.

Networks and coalitions are other ways in which diplomats try to manage our uncertain and volatile world. Contact networks provide crucial information about what is going on while offering the chance to influence key actors. They offer the chance to engage with a broad range of other actors, listening as well as speaking, bad actors as well as good actors. It is this engagement which distinguishes diplomacy from other activities like lobbying and public relations. Diplomacy recognizes that the other has a voice and a world view that may differ from yours but is sincerely held and valid in his eyes. This diplomatic empathy – the ability to see the world and your actions through the eyes of the other – lies at the core of traditional diplomacy and at the heart of network-building. If we talk to, and take seriously, only those we agree with, we condemn ourselves to an echo chamber which will distort how we understand the world while failing to influence broader geopolitical debates. Sadly, this seems to be the fate of much Western diplomacy today. The importance of engaging with those unlike you is shown clearly in coalition-building. Effective coalitions include heterogenous members brought together by shared preferred outcomes rather than shared values or ideologies. In the words of Churchill, the only thing worse than fighting a war with allies is fighting one without them (Roberts, 2019). And his allies included Stalin's Soviet Union. Building coalitions only with those who share our values limits their extent and effectiveness. If, on the other hand, we can build coalitions including actors who do not agree with us on everything but do share a preferred outcome on the one area the coalition is focused on, then we are more likely to secure our objectives. The heterogenous coalitions of companies, governments, and NGOs, tied together by preferred outcomes rather than values, were crucial to securing the Paris Accords on climate change. For companies, this means that market competitors may be allies in managing geopolitical risk. This because companies that compete within a given sector face the common geopolitical risks of that sector. They share an interest in developing and protecting that sector even while competing within it.

Bruno Maçães (2025) recently suggested that in an age of advanced technology, geopolitics is not so much a contest to control territory as to create the territory. Great powers seek to build worlds in which other states have to live. The WTO was an attempt by the United States to construct a trade free world in which other states would have to operate. The protocols and operating rules of the internet were created in the United States and then imposed on the rest of the world at a moment of U.S. hegemony. U.S. efforts to expel Huawei from 5G telephone infrastructure resulted as much from U.S. concerns about the company's role in setting 5G's international industrial standards as concerns about data security. Meta/Facebook strives to set the rules of the Metaverse. Multiple states compete to set the rules and protocols for AI. The irruption of geopolitics into virtual worlds may seem to endanger our definition of geopolitics as the political meaning or interpretation of geography. But virtual worlds have their own geography: the internet has the physical infrastructure of data storage and sub-oceanic cables, as well as the virtual geography of the world wide web, both defining its vulnerabilities to attack; AI depends on vulnerable supply chains of critical minerals and microprocessors, both open to political manipulation, as well as dependence on large quantities of water and energy. Other analysts speak of a bounded world order, in which great powers like China and the United States will create their own distinct world orders in which their allies will trade, effectively bifurcating world trade and finance (Shearing, 2025). A more plausible alternative might be asymmetric multipolarity, in which there are two superpowers (China and the United States), but no hegemon or bifurcation of the world order. Medium size power like India, Turkey, or Saudi Arabia as well as countries in Europe and Southeast Asia have considerable freedom to pursue their national interests as they perceive them, working together with whichever other powers best suit their interests. Such a system would be a world of fluid and dynamic alliances built around specific shared interests or shared preferred outcomes. As Palmerston said in the 19th century, very much a world of asymmetric multipolarity, countries have no permanent friends or enemies, only permanent interests. Whatever new world order emerges, it will be an unpredictable and bumpy ride as we travel from the old to the new. Companies will need to adopt and adapt the skills, techniques, and mindsets of diplomacy to navigate choppy and threatening waters. We believe that learning from the diplomats can help.

During the summer of 2024, Chinese EV companies were increasingly concerned about the prospect of the European Commission imposing tariffs on the import of Chinese EVs into the EU. They relied on their government and direct lobbying of the Commission to persuade the EU not to impose the tariffs. The Commission proposed to impose tariffs of between 8% and 35%, and this was adopted by the member states. As we have seen, sometimes your government is part of the problem. Relations between the Commission and the Chinese government were at a low ebb at the time. Was there an alternative business diplomacy approach that might have been more successful? The proposal to impose the tariffs by the Commission was only adopted by the member states by a minority vote (the majority abstained, and several voted against). This suggests that there was a possibility of convincing the member states to reject the proposal, which was unpopular with different sectors within the EU. The German government feared retaliation against German cars in China. Environmentalists were concerned about the impact on the Green Transition and Net Zero. Other governments worried about their broader trade relations with China. The elements existed to construct an effective heterogenous coalition around the shared preferred outcome of no tariffs on Chinese EVs. Each participant would have had its own reasons for belonging to the coalition with the shared preferred outcome creating the coalition's coherence. A business diplomacy approach may have led to a better outcome.

References

Gewen, B. (2020). *The inevitability of tragedy: Henry Kissinger and his world*. Norton.

Gorodetsky, G. (2015). *The Maisky Diaries: Red Ambassador to the Court of St James's, 1932–1943*. Yale University Press.

Kaplan, R. D. (2012). *The revenge of geography: What the map tells us about coming conflicts and the battle against fate*. Random House.

Maçães, B. (2025). *World builders: Technology and the new geopolitics*. Cambridge University Press.

Murphy, D. T. (1997). *The heroic earth: Geopolitical thought in Weimar Germany, 1918–1933*. Kent State University Press.

Roberts, A. (2019). *Churchill: Walking with destiny*. Penguin.

Sharp, P. (2009). *Diplomatic theory of international relations*. Cambridge University Press.

Shearing, N. (2025). *The fractured age: How the return of geopolitics will splinter the global economy*. John Murray Business.

Smeets, M. (2025). *Ransom war: How cyber crime became a threat to national security*. Hurst Publishers.

Index

Note: Page numbers in *italics* indicate figures, and page numbers in **bold** indicate tables in the text.